TWO SHORT-SLEEVED ONES AND A SWEATSHIRT

A Victim No More

Pamela Devereueawax

PAGE PUBLISHING
Conneaut Lake, PA

First originally published by Page Publishing 2023

ISBN 979-8-88793-828-8 (pbk)
ISBN 979-8-88793-830-1 (digital)

Printed in the United States of America

This book is dedicated to my three beautiful daughters, the most amazing gifts this life has given me. You are my Angels, may you know I unconditionally love you!

CHAPTER ONE

Secrets

Secrets, I became a master at keeping them, so much so that I even kept them from myself.

I was wearing a light-green dress with white ruffles, white socks with lace to match the ruffles on my dress, and white patent leather shoes. My mom sat me on the tan leather examining table as she stood beside me talking to the old man in the white coat. The man in the white coat then turned away to pick something up from a shiny tray behind him, and when he turned back to face me, he had a silver knife in his hand. All of a sudden, my mom held my arms and legs down so that I couldn't move, what's happening, what are they doing to me? I'm so scared, I started to scream and crying as he came closer with the knife. The next thing I remember I was walking out of the doctor's office with a sucker in one hand, my mom's hand in the other, and a chin and neck full of Band-Aids. I looked up at my mom and asked, "I was good girl, wasn't I, Mommy"? This was my first childhood memory, in its entirety. I had been diagnosed with skin cancer at the age of three, and my mom had taken me to the physician's office to have it removed. The doctor did not use any type of anesthetic, not even a topical one and the silver knife, was a scalpel. That was my first memorable dissociative experience, a survival technique I had perfected already at the age of three.

I was born on a cold winter day in January 1973. My mother and father were married the year prior and were anxiously awaiting my coming into the world. This was the year the Vietnam war would finally come to an end, the endangered species act was passed, Roe vs Wade made abortion legal, and hip-hop was born. The Rolling Stones were at the top of the charts. The Sears Tower was completed as well as tower two of the World Trade Center, making it the tallest building in the world. This era was deemed the "Me" generation. Woman's rights, desegregation, and gay pride were making headlines daily. So much positive change, but where there is good, there is also evil. These were also the times when people minded their own business; and what happened behind closed doors, stayed behind closed doors. The punishment for animal abuse was more severe than that of child abuse. Unfortunately, child abuse was not talked about. It was kept a secret. Kept secret by both the abuser and the abused; therefore, the minimal punishment available was rarely carried out. As a result, none of my abusers were ever held accountable, let alone prosecuted for their crimes against me and thus rings true for countless numbers of innocent children all over the world. It has taken me forty-four years to break my silence and to tell my secrets. This has been a long grueling journey for me. I have been to hell and back time and again and have taken the ones I love with me. I have done many things I'm not proud of and am extremely embarrassed to divulge, but I know that I am not alone. I am ready to be free from the horrors of my past, ready to heal, and ready to move forward to a beautiful place. It is my mission to reach as many victims of abuse as I possibly can and move them to break their silence. As long as these secrets are kept, we will remain victims; and this vicious cycle will continue.

Abusers come in all shapes and sizes. There is no *typical* type. They are male and female, young and old alike, and multitudes of nationalities. Child predators are our next-door neighbors, respected members of our community, and mostly, people we trust. In my case, it was my father. This is my story, although it may be unbelievable at times. It is all true.

I was raised in a middle-class home. My parents were married, and both were employed full-time. My father was a professional painter, and my mother an insurance adjuster. I was given all the material things I ever wanted, but so much more was stolen from me. From the outside in it looked perfect, but I had a secret. Such a horrifying secret, I learned to keep it from myself. I'm going to take you on a journey through my life. This journey will move all your emotions and make you feel uncomfortable in your own skin. What I ask is that you complete this journey with me and share it with as many people as possible. Chances are, if you are reading this, you yourself have been affected by some form of abuse or someone you know has. I want everyone who has been impacted, in any way shape or form by abuse to know, that there is life beyond being a victim. I want to share my gift of becoming a survivor, and let those who have been affected by this epidemic know that there is a beautiful, fulfilling, and loving life out there waiting for you. I promise that when you let your secrets go, you will begin to heal. I invite you to embark on this voyage with me, to ride the waves of my life; and when you disembark, you take something with you. That something is hope. Let us now begin. Take my hand and walk beside me.

My mom was a working mother, and six weeks after my birth, it was time for her to go back to work. She asked one of her fellow employees and close friends of hers, who she would recommend to care for me. Upon this recommendation, I was taken to this woman's home to be cared for while my parents were at work. One evening after work, my mom pulled up to the babysitter's house. Upon arriving, she could hear my bloodcurdling screams coming from the house. Mind you, its winter; so all the windows and doors were closed due to the cold. As she entered the home and approached the bassinette I was in, she found broken glass shattered all around me on the sheets and blanket I was covered with. She never took me back there. She also never asked what happened, nor did she call the police to report the incident. Desperate for someone to care for her newborn baby, she reached out to a friend whom she trusted, Roseanne. At first, she said she was unable to care for me. She was working and in school. After my mom told her the story of what had happened with the babysitter, Roseanne spoke with her family; and they agreed to help care for me. This kindhearted, amazing family were among my first angels. They would care for me five days a week for the next five years. They loved me and treated me like their own. I became part of their family. They helped me feel *normal*, gave me a good example of what a family was supposed to be like. Unfortunately, I never confided in them about the horrors that were happening at my house and other places I was being taken. As a matter of fact, the only questionable thing about my behavior was that I never wanted to go home. I would cry and plead to stay with her. I was a good girl though, good at keeping the secrets because I knew if I told, I would be punished or cut or killed.

Often on the weekends, we would go to my maternal grandparents' home an hour south west of where we lived. All of my mother's family lived here. It wouldn't be out of the ordinary for all of us younger children to be babysat by the older ones while the sisters went out shopping. On one such occasion upon arriving back to my aunt's home, my mom walked in the basement where she caught my sixteen-year-old female cousin French-kissing me. When she asked her what she was doing, she replied, "I was practicing." I was two years old. My mom did nothing to protect me, but what she did do was continue to let me be babysat on the weekends by my cousins and sometimes their father. I can remember playing games like peek-a-boo and hide-and-seek, but these games were not the ones you imagine when you hear their names.

Peek-a-boo was reinvented. It went something like this. I would have to close and cover my eyes with my hands like in peek-a-boo; but when I opened them, one of my cousins both male and female would be exposing their private parts to me. Putting them in my face. They smelled bad. Then there was hide-and-seek. In this reinvented version, I would have to hide; and if I was found, I had to perform sex acts on my cousins, or let them touch my private parts. I was always found. Sometimes, when I was found, I was taken to my uncle so he could do what he wanted with me. I can remember the look and smell of the soiled sheets in his bedroom. It would make me gag and cough the smell of must was so bad, at least my daddy didn't stink. This continued until I was old enough to stay home alone and refused to go over there. I never told. I kept the secret because I was told to, and I had already been taught by my father what could happen if I shared my secrets.

It's early Sunday morning and time to get ready for church. I'm in my bedroom getting dressed. I put my red and black plaid skirt on, and I am buttoning up my white short sleeved shirt when Daddy comes in and tells me not to wear underwear today. I'm sitting in the back seat of the car on my way to church. I don't understand why I'm not supposed to wear underwear. I feel weird. I'll just keep my skirt pulled down, and no one will notice. Okay, here we go. Ah, church, all the pretty windows with pictures of Jesus and the lambs. It makes me feel happy when I'm here. We get up to our same place we always sit in, left side toward the middle. The pews are so neat with crosses in the ends of them. Mommy goes in first. I'm holding her hand, and Daddy follows behind me. We are all sitting down. The music begins to play. That means church is about to start. I'm looking around at how big everything is and pretty, but my bare butt on these seats itches. Pastor comes out, so we all stand up. Daddy whispers something to Mommy. She lifts up my skirt and sees I don't have underwear on. Mommy said, "Why don't you have panties on? You know better." Before I could say anything, my daddy scooped me up in his arms and told my mom he would take me home to put them on. As he steps out of the pew with me in his arms, I stand in the aisle and watch the man walk away with the little girl until they disappear out the big doors into the sunlight. I then go back and sit with my mommy where I am safe. I feel sad because I know where she is going. She goes so I don't have to. She goes so I am safe. She goes so we can keep our secret and so that we don't have to die and get put in the attic. We are four years old.

As I mentioned previously, by the age of three, I had mastered the art of dissociation. It's a coping mechanism where I separated myself from the trauma I was under-going. Let me explain. The sexual abuse was happening on such a regular basis that my little developing brain could not take it, but what it could do was develop a tool to help me survive it. When it was too much for me to handle, I just separated myself from the situation. I could watch myself and then leave. I went someplace safe and happy, and she took the abuse.

When it was over. I came back. Just like autopilot on an airplane, it's as easy as a flip of a switch. I say, it is because I use this coping mechanism to this day.

My father was a monster, a very charming, deceptive, and intelligent beast. He used a combination of threats, punishment, and grooming to make me keep our secret. Yes, my father was a pedophile, a child abuser in every way imaginable. This man who was supposed to be my protector, my inspiration, and my god, tortured me. I was molested on a frequent and regular basis. He made me his sex toy, molded me just the way he wanted me. It started at a very young age. I never knew anything was wrong about it. I just thought that's what daddies did with their daughters; or better yet from all my experience, that's what little girls did for men.

In the beginning he taught me, taught me how to sit on his lap with no panties on so he could play between my legs. How to unzip his pants, pull his penis out, and put it in my mouth. He was nice about it, coaching me, telling me it was okay, telling me it felt good, making it a game.

I distinctly remember the incident that made me realize that what was going on was not right.

It's Thanksgiving Day, the whole family is at our house to eat turkey. All my aunts, uncles, and cousins are here. The house is so busy. After dinner, all the men go to the basement to watch football and drink beer. While the women clean up, drink coffee, and gossip. One of my teenage male cousins is sitting on the couch in the basement. This is the couch Daddy and I always play on. I crawl up on the couch. I'm sitting next to him, and I laid my head on his belly and start to unzip his pants, like I do with Daddy, but my cousin didn't like it. He pushed me off him, and said, "No! What are you doing?" It was at that moment I knew what was happening between my father and I was wrong. I felt sad, angry, and embarrassed. He had seen what I did, and I would pay for that later. I'm five years old.

Everyone had gone home from the Thanksgiving feast. I was all tucked in bed with my PJs on ready for sleep to come when Daddy came in my room. I knew he was coming for me because I saw his shadow in my night-light. He got me out of my bed and made me walk through the kitchen to the top of the basement stairs as he followed behind me. As I started to take my first step down, my feet came out from underneath me; and I tumbled down the uncarpeted, red, wood stairs on to a cement floor. I had been kicked. When my daddy got to the bottom of the stairs, he stood over me and with his mouth squinched up as he placed his hand over my mouth to stop me from crying. He said to me, "Quit your fucking crying, or I will kill you. Now go get your ass on that couch like I taught you. I'm going to teach you a lesson now." I'm so scared, so very, very scared. I run to the couch as fast as I can. As the morning sun began to peek through my window, I stretch in my bed. Mmmm, I smell the coffee. That means Mommy is up! I am sitting on the toilet going potty, and it hurts. I'm all red down there. It's so bad, dark red, on my belly and legs. How am I going to hide this? I don't want to die. If I dare tell anyone, he will kill me. I know because he tells me so, all the time.

This was the first time I can remember my father using physical violence to punish me and keep me under control. When I say physical, I mean brutal. I was used to the usual threats of cutting me, killing me, etc. I had also become accustom to being slapped in the face, not only with my father's hands but other articles, such as rolled-up newspapers, magazines, and shoes. I think his favorite was kicking me as I would walk by because it was like a game. He had to be able to hit a moving target. I can remember being picked up by my neck and choked while my little feet dangled in the air then being dropped to the floor and gasping for air. Sometimes it was a combination of being choaked and beaten in the face at the same time. I have some memories of the day to day regular physical, emotional, and sexual abuse. It's when it got brutal, and I couldn't handle it that she took over. I'm not sure if I have an alternate personality, but I have the little girl who took the brutal abuse that I couldn't, locked away inside my head, I call her Suzzie after my middle name Sue. She is my hero.

On the flip side of my nightmarish life, there was a never-ending supply of lavish gifts and anything I wanted. That's right! I was presented to the world by my father as a *spoiled brat* who got anything she wanted. This is one thing he did not lie about. I did have everything I asked for and more. My own toy/play room, filled with every new toy available, yearly trips to Santa's Village, and Disney World, the biggest best Christmas ever! I was given it all, but there was a price. The price for me was my innocence. This act of gift giving is called grooming. I was given all these gifts in exchange for silence. I was given everything I ever wanted so I would keep my secret. Guess what, it worked. With the combination of grooming and violence, I never told, not a soul. My father was a very smart but evil man. And he had already had years of practice before I was brought into this world. Yes, I said years. By the time I came around, he had learned from his mistakes and perfected his craft of manipulation and abuse. I will tell you more about that later.

We often vacationed with my parents friends in Michigan. They had a set of log cabins on a lake up there. Some of my best memories are here. I was free when I was here. He didn't touch me when we were here because there were too many people around. I love the forest, the wild animals, swimming in the lake, and fishing. This place was my safe haven. I could run, play, be wild, and free.

One morning, I wake up early before everyone else. It's just getting light outside. I feel like going fishing, so I get dressed and go potty. I'm real quiet so I don't wake anyone up. I sneak out the door of the cabin and head down to the lake. I get my fishing pole and some worms from the boat house, put my life jacket on, and push the row boat out into the water, and jump in. I use the oars to paddle out further into the lake so I can fish and cast my line. It's so quiet. I like it out here. I am five years old.

Also at the age of five, I was taken from Roseanne's home where I was loved and hugged and placed in preschool at We Care Day Care Center. The stories are conflicting about why my mom took me from them and put me in day care, but I believe it was to protect my father. I remember vividly my first day there. Mommy and I pulled up to my new school, look at all the toys outside, jungle jims, swings, tunnels, oh boy! We get out of the car, and Mommy is holding my hand while we walk inside. There lots of other kids playing. I'm not used to all that activity, but everyone is having fun. Tom and Jerry is playing on a TV in the room where all the kids are playing. There are lots of tables and chairs some kids are coloring. Maybe I will like it here like Mommy says. Everything seems okay and then a male teacher comes and says hi to me. Why is a man here? I don't want a man here. Men hurt me, no, no, no. I scream and cry and hold on to Mommy tight. "Don't leave me with a man. No, Mommy, no. Please don't leave me alone with this man. Please, Mommy, please." I associated men with violence, fear, and pain. The thought of being in the care of another man had sent me into panic-stricken frenzy. It took them a half hour to calm me down. I still didn't tell my secret.

At the age of six, it was time for elementary school. Like I said, I was given everything, including a private school education. Saint Paul Lutheran is the name of my school. It is also the church I've attended since birth. On my first day of school, Mommy and Daddy took me; and we had a meeting with the principal, Mr. Snodgrass. He is a tall older man with white hair sitting behind a big wooden desk. The three of us sit down opposite of him. He's talking to my parents, and I'm looking around his office. I see a big board with a handle and holes in it, hanging by a piece of rope on the wall; and it had writing on it "board of education," scary. My parents are looking at papers and signing them, talking back and forth with Mr. Snodgrass when he stands up and takes this board off the wall. He then begins to tell me how my mommy and daddy just signed a permission slip that said, if I was a bad girl at school, he could spank me with that board that had holes in it, and that it would hurt real bad; so I better be good. True story. I was always good at schoolwork but not so much at school.

Every morning, we started our day with the Pledge of Allegiance to our flag. We all stood up, faced the flag, placed our right hand over our heart, and recited the pledge. After completing the pledge, we took our seats, and it was time for morning prayer. Our desks were the kind that had the seat connected. They were metal on the bottom with a heavy wooden top that opened up. This particular morning, I had a cold, and my nose was running. I had my eyes closed for prayer, and I tried sneaking my hand in my desk to get a Kleenex because snot was going into my mouth. Wham! Bam, bam, bam, bam. My first-grade teacher, Mrs. Snodgrass, had caught me sneaking in my desk. I had my eyes closed for prayer, so I didn't see her coming, so I didn't get my hands out fast enough. She repeatedly smashed the heavy wooden desk top on my little six-year-old hands. By the time school was out for the day, my hands were all black and blue. I did not go home and tell my parents what she had done. My mom discovered the bruising and asked me what had happened. I was not taken for medical treatment that I recall. When my parents found out what happened to my hands, my dad went to the principal's office. Nothing ever happened because you see, the principal was the first-grade teacher's husband. By the time I was seven years old, I saw the world as a scary, mean, angry place. I had endured so much pain and suffering that I became angry too. I was getting into fistfights on a regular basis at school. I couldn't control how I was treated at home, but I refused to let people my own size hurt me.

The physical, sexual and emotional abuse my father dealt out was relentless and dealt out on a regular basis. Day in and day out, week after week, year after year, with only Suzzie to save me. I just kept the secrets. I was so brainwashed into believing I would be killed if I told. All these people around me, and no one noticed what was going on. When I was six or seven, my mom's youngest sister came to live with us for a while. She was attending college in our home town, so it saved her dorm fees. My parents made a room for her in the attic. It was one of those attics that had a stairwell leading up to it. One night, I asked my aunt if I could sleep up there with her; and she said yes. She really said yes! I slept in that bed with my aunt every night I possibly could. With her there, it was harder for him to get to me. She didn't even know, but she was my angel. I wanted so badly for someone to see, just to open their eyes and save me; but the help never came because I was too afraid to ask for it. Too trained to keep my secret. So I took advantage of small miracles when they presented themselves. Other than that, I had to figure it out on my own; so I did. I employed things from my surroundings to help me deal with the daily torture I endured from my father, I call them my tools.

CHAPTER TWO

Toolbox

Now that you have a glimpse into my childhood, it is important that you know how I survived. I learned how to adapt to my surroundings. There was never a time I felt safe. I lived in a state of constant fear, fear of my father. He was so big, angry, and mean; and I was his only target. He took his frustrations out on me. He satisfied his sexual urges with my body. He was like a time bomb waiting to explode at any moment. It was like I constantly walked on egg shells, dodged land mines, and ran for cover. I was held at gunpoint and threatened with knives being held to my throat. It was like being in combat. I didn't have anyone to comfort me, to tell me it was over. I had no one to save me and tell me everything was going to be okay. I lived in a war zone and I had to figure it out how to survive on my own.

One of the first tools I used to sooth myself was to suck my thumb. I sucked my left thumb and used my forefinger to rub my upper lip. I did this until I got married at twenty-two.

In order to survive, I developed coping mechanisms and used my surroundings to help me the best I could. I call them my tools. Many of them were by no means healthy ways to cope, but it was all I had and didn't know any better. There was, to some degree, when I was little, my mom would rub my back when I was falling asleep and hugged me sometimes; I can remember. She turned her back to what was happening and never attempted to save me. You see, I wasn't being raised in a loving nurturuturing home where I was being shown affection. It was quite the opposite. I was being raised with no boundaries, being taught what was evil was good or at least normal. As I grew, I realized I wasn't normal, my family wasn't normal; and I couldn't tell a soul. Even though there were people all around me, I felt so alone.

Now, I can't tell you for sure if Suzzie came first as an imaginary friend because I was so alone or if she came to save me from the abuse first and then became my friend. Either way, I made her; and she became a part of me. At first, I only used her as a last resort. I would take as much as I could from this man called my father. When it got to be more than I could comprehend and handle, Suzzie took over. She became my protector, my defense, my guard, and one of my many Angels. I'm pretty sure she gave my dad a run for his money because there have been times in my life that I have been present while Suzzie was out. She is a feisty and fiery little girl. At first, she didn't have a name. She was just the other little girl who would come to take my spot when I couldn't deal with what was happening to me. Because I was an only child at this point, she was my best friend. We had tea parties and played school together. Oh, the fun we had! Turning rocks over in the backyard to find the bugs, making mud pies, and jumping in the puddles when it had rained. She was always with me as our friendship grew. I didn't feel so alone.

I absolutely loved Raggedy Ann! I had the doll, the books, the dress; and my mom even made me a ceramic one for decoration in my room. She was a rag doll with bright red yarn for hair and black buttons for eyes. Her clothing consisted of a light blue flower print dress and a white apron. Man, I loved me some Raggedy Ann, woo hoo! She was the bee's knees. I took her everywhere with me. We spent hours playing together every day. Oh yeah! Raggedy Ann was the name of the doll, the brand per say; but I called her Suzzie. She became so much a part of me. As I became an adult, although being of Irish descent and having red highlights in my hair, I started coloring it red on a frequent and regular basis.

Let's talk about my surroundings. I lived in a two-bedroom, one-bathroom house. It was white with brown trim. There were three steps up to the front porch door. The front porch was enclosed and had windows with screens. From the front porch was the main entry into the house. Upon entering is the living room, which then opens to the dining room. The attic was finished and accessible from the dining room. Off the dining room to the right was a hallway containing the bathroom and a bedroom on each side. My parents' room was at the front of the house adjacent to the living room, and my room was at the back of the house. The kitchen was off the dining room going straight back, and the basement stairs were adjacent to the kitchen. The back door entrance was at the top of the basement stairs; so if entering from the back door, you could either go down the stairs to the basement or up three steps to enter the kitchen. There were ten wooden stairs leading to the basement that were painted red. The landing was cement, painted gray. On each side of the landing, there was a room. To the left was the laundry room, and to the right were my dad's tools and workbench. It had peg board on the wall behind the workbench where he hung miscellaneous tools. Right in the middle was a big fish head on a plaque with its mouth open like it was coming to eat me. I was terrified of that fish, my dad found it funny. Going forward is a *family room*. The walls are lined with wood-grain paneling, and the floors are covered in rainbow shag carpet. There is a brown and white floral-patterned couch, two multi-colored, vertically-striped velvet swivel lounge chairs, and a 19-inch tube television. Walk to the back of this room and to the left is my toy room, paneled walls and shag carpet as well. It is a continuation of the family room, a nook, if you will. It has a half wall with a large cut out for a window, but there is no glass for the entryway. I'm describing my home in such detail for you because the house itself became a tool for my survival.

My room was the smaller of the two. It had two windows. One was by the closet. The other by my bed. My dresser was in the corner with my raggedy ann, my mom made in ceramics and a night-light. My mom made my night-light in ceramics as well. It's a brown-haired little girl wearing a yellow dress and yellow bonnet to match. She is sitting on a hill. The dress and bonnet have holes all over in them to let the light shine through.

Many nights, my mommy and daddy stay up and watch TV after I go to bed. Sometimes Mommy goes to bed before Daddy, and he stays up watching TV. I can hear him coming, he leaves the TV on. Maybe he will just go into the bathroom. I pull the covers over my head and leave one eye out so I can see the balls of light coming from the night-light. I can see if he's coming cause of the shadow over the balls of light. When he pulls down my covers, I try to pretend I'm sleeping; and maybe he will leave me alone; but no, instead he sits down on the side of my bed. While my daddy is pulling up my night gown and pulling down my panties, he runs his hard fingers over my chest. I watch the balls of light on the wall. They are pretty. I count them. I count them up and down, back and forth. I count and count and count them until he is done.

Sometimes he would be slow in coming and walking funny. He was like that when he drank more beer then I could run and hide in my closet. I'm safe. I scooch all the way back in the corner, and I listen, and I wait. I put my hand over my mouth so he can't hear me breathe. I leave the door open a little so I can still see the balls of light. I'll know if he's coming for me that way. I can get ready. I can get little. He doesn't find me all the time. Sometimes he sleeps on my bed, and I sleep in the closet all night. Allow me to explain *getting little*. It's a tool I used where I wished myself little by reciting *get little* over and over again until poof! I was gone. I believe this was the beginning stage of me creating Suzzie.

I was aware of my suroundings at all times. I had to be ready for anything. I found hiding places: in the dryer, behind curtains, under dirty clothes, my toy box, the closet in the attic upstairs. Sometimes they worked; but most times, I was only putting off the inevitable. One of his favorite places to molest me was on the couch, which was located in the family room in the basement. I learned to use the basement stairs as a tool. I learned to hold the handrail as I descended the ten stairs, holding on kept me from falling when he would try to kick me down them. I would also count them as I walked, trying to go slow to waste time because I knew what was going to happen when my feet hit the cold concrete floor beneath me; and I made my way across the room to the couch. So I would count one step, two steps, three steps, four, almost halfway. What am I going to do? If I run, he will catch me; and it will be worse than just playing with Daddy. Step 5, I can't run now. There is no way out. Step 6, I feel his hand on the back of my head pushing me forward. Step 7, someone please save me. Please, please save me. Step 8, step 9, step 10; and just as my right root hits the cold gray concrete floor, poof! I'm gone. Suzzie heard me. She didn't always hear my cries and save me, but she saved me many, many times in my childhood.

As I grew older, I developed new tools. Suzzie and I didn't play as much. I didn't need her as much at least that's what I thought. I had found a tool that worked, food. I could control my world with food. It was the only thing I had that made me feel good. I would sneak food whenever I got a chance. I hid it in my room so I could eat late at night. Sometimes I would sneak in the fridge after they went to sleep. I soon realized that the more I ate, the bigger I became, and the less my dad was attracted to me. Now with the weight gain came a whole new realm of verbal abuse, but guess what? I didn't care. I was just glad he wasn't touching me sexually all the time. I fell in love with food! Food was my savior! It hurt that my dad called me fat, chubby; and he smacked my mouth when I ate wrong. It didn't stop me, but the price I had to pay just to get a reprieve from the sexual abuse at home would be a big one. Yes, I was the chubby kid in class, Miss Piggy, fat-fat-fatty, chunky checker, if you can think it. I was called it and for many years. As I got older, I became bulimic. I learned that I could still get the comfort from eating the food but not have to gain the weight. I would eat and eat and eat until I felt like I could explode, making sure I drank a lot too. I learned that drinking a lot while binging made purging easier. I would starve myself for days and then binge and purge, and it would cycle like that. It didn't matter how much weight I gained or lost. No matter what I did, my body never really felt like my own. Often times the image I saw in the mirror did not match the image I remembered.

Even though I was teased about my weight, I didn't let that stop me. I excelled in school. I gave it my all and very early on. It became one of my tools. I was always on the honor roll. I had perfect attendance the majority of the time. I was in every extracurricular activity there was available. I fell in love with volleyball, and I excelled in it. Our team made it to the championships! We were sectioned out to A and B teams. The B team being the girls that weren't as good. I was placed on the B team because I was the fat girl. Well, I showed them! I served an entire fifteen point game single handedly. When it came time to hand out trophies, I was shocked when my name was called to receive a most valuable player trophy. As they presented it to me, the announcer said that I by no means should have been on that B team; and I deserved this trophy more than anyone on the team. That was the first time I had ever felt like somebody. Outside of school, I was in ballet, tumbling, pom poms, and swimming lessons. The more I was involved in school, the less I had to be at home. The less I had to be at home, the less I was tortured. Even though I was being teased and bullied at school, it was better than what I was dealing with at home. I loved school and hated it at the same time.

As I said earlier, the tools I used were by no means healthy ones. The older I became, the more unhealthy my coping mechanisms became. The first time I tried to commit suicide, I was ten years old. I sat on the cold white tiled bathroom floor with a bottle of Tylenol in one hand and a glass of orange juice in the other. I put the bottle up to my mouth, tipped my head back, and dumped a bunch in and washed them down with the juice. I repeated this three times until the bottle was gone with the hope that I wouldn't wake up in the morning. It didn't work, but that didn't stop me from trying. I tried again at age fourteen. My mom figured out I had taken pills because I was acting funny. When she asked me if I had taken too much medicine, I told her I had. That was my first experience with getting my stomach pumped and an overnight stay in the hospital. They put a tube into my nose that went down into my stomach so that they could pump activated charcoal in to absorb the pills. I can remember lying in that cold hard bed. My throat raw from the tube. I had a roommate, an elderly woman who was moaning and crying out all night. I prayed to god and promised I would never do it again, but I lied. It's sad that I cannot give you an exact count on the number of times I tried to escape the pain of my life by removing myself from this world. My guess is around thirty or forty, give or take a few.

There are times I tried to commit suicide that I have no memory of. I found out by reading about it in my journals or from going through my medical records to write this book.

At the age of nineteen, my mother took me to an attorney, had a last will and testament drawn up, had me sign it, and had it notarized. It was my last will and testament, not hers. I will elaborate more in future chapters, I'm introducing it now because attempting suicide became a tool I used. A form of escape. An escape from all my secrets. I just didn't see a way out from underneath the darkness. I was ashamed of myself. I didn't like myself. As a matter of fact, I hated myself. Why should I keep suffering in this life when I could just stop the suffering. I could just go to sleep and not wake up, and the pain would be gone forever. I relentlessly tried to end my life, attempting suicide over and over, and over again. I am only here today because my angels were watching out for me. Please understand I am not afraid of death. I never have been. All the times I heard in school or church that those who commit suicide go to hell, didn't stop me; and I didn't care. When it is my time and death comes, I will welcome it. It is only because I know that this physical life I am living now is only a small part of my journey.

I was eleven or twelve when I started self-mutilating. It started innocently at school with writing on my arm with an eraser. I took the pencil and turned it around and rubbed it against my skin until it peeled off, eraser burn. I was instantly in love with the feeling of pain. Let me explain. The feeling of physical pain that inflicted on myself took away the emotional pain that I was enduring. It was a release, and a new tool I added to my box. After erasers, came paper clips. I would scratch my arms with the ends of paper clips until I drew blood. I also tried butter knives then steak knives; and one day, I came across razor blades on my dad's workbench. A cut from a razor blade burns first and then comes the pain. That's the feeling I was looking for. I cut myself frequently because it worked for me. It temporarily stopped the noise inside my head. It gave me a feeling of calm and peace. I cut myself up so badly one time, it ended me up in the children's psychiatric unit for six weeks. I was sixteen, I never told my secret even when I was in a safe place with people to help me. Self-mutilation is tool. I continued to use throughout the years.

By the age of twelve, I was masturbating multiple times a night before I would go to sleep. In fact, I wasn't able to fall asleep without masturbating. I'm pretty sure it was because of all the years of my father coming in my room at night and doing it to me before I fell asleep. I took it further than just digital stimulation. I experimented with inserting different objects into my vagina. Sometimes the things I used would make me bleed. I had trouble telling the difference between the sensations of pleasure and pain. At some point, I began cutting myself with razor blades and masturbating together.

I'm downstairs in the new house in the family room. I'm wearing my white night gown with a big figment on it that I got from our last trip to Disney World. I have panties on but no bra. I retrieve a razor blade from my stash in my room, turn on a soft porn movie on show time, and settle in the big blue leather recliner. I'm thirteen years old. It is also at this age I became curious about the stash of liquor kept in our basement and beer kept in our refrigerator. I sneaked sips here and there. I liked how it made me feel a warm and fuzzy; and most of all, I liked the way it made me not feel anything.

One weekend night, I had a friend spend the night. She brought baby food jars over, and we went to the booze shelf in the basement. We proceeded to pour different kinds of alcohol, all together in these two jars. We went to my room and started taking shots. After a little while, we sneaked out the back door with the other jar and began roaming around the neighborhood. We finished the other jar while out walking around. We went to a local restaurant that had a cigarette machine to try to buy a pack. We were wasted. A car full of high school boys tried to get us into a car with them, but we didn't. We ended up at one of our fellow student's houses whose father was also an influential member of the board at our school. So here my friend and I are outside in the front yard of this boy's home, throwing rocks at his window, hanging from the tree, and yelling out to get his attention. Well, we got more than his attention. We got his father's as well. Luckily, I had thought ahead and took the home phone off the hook, just in case. He put our drunk thirteen-year-old butts in the back seat of his car and tried to call my parents, but it was busy. He attempted to drive us home, and I lied and had him pull up to someone else's house two blocks away. When he got out and went up to these poor unsuspecting peoples home and knocked on their door at two in the morning, I grabbed my friend; and we jumped out of the back seat and hauled ass across the street and down the creek that ran behind all the houses on my street. Yes, we did. All the way back to my house, and we made it. It wasn't until sometime later, after we had passed out and puked all over my water bed, did her parents show up at my parents' house. This was my first drunken experience and another tool to add to my box.

Using alcohol made me feel good; but when I was introduced to drugs, those made me feel great. The first time I used drugs, it was with my cousin. I'm not sure how the whole thing got started, but we crushed up some pills and snorted them up. After the pill snorting, we had sex. I was unsure of what to do because I had never done it with a girl before, but she instructed me. You see, she has her own story too. That is how she knew what to do. I am thirteen years old.

Now I'm not sure how I got the sack of weed, or how I even rolled a joint because I can't roll one to save my life now. But what I do know is that I got it, and I did it. Not only that, but I got my mom to drop me off at my friends place of employment with it. I walked my butt right into that McDonald's, went straight to the bathroom, took a seat on the toilet in one of the stalls, and lit that sucker up. Yes, I got high in a McDonald's bathroom, not any McDonald's. The one my friend was working at and was getting ready to finish up her shift so we could go *study*. After I was good and high, I put it out, flushed the toilet, washed my hands, and made my way to the front of the store to wait on my friend to finish her shift. It was going to be a few minutes, so I sat down on a bench across from the front counter. I was so thirsty, and I could hardly see out of my eyes when my friend came up and handed me her car keys. She could smell the weed on me, and someone had smelled it in the bathroom. She asked me if I had smoked in there, to which I replied, "Hell yes." I took the keys and waited for her in the car. I was fifteen years old.

Once I started using drugs, it was a whole new escape. I used speed and marijuana on a regular basis, but I would try anything that came my way. The only drug I never tried was heroin. PCP, LSD, prescription medications from my parent's medicine cupboard. You name it. I did it and never thought twice about it. I had finally found a tool to become comfortably numb. There are countless stories of my escapades while on drugs, but there are a few that I would like to share.

One New Year's Eve, a couple of my friends came over; and we took a few hits of acid. We spent the night coloring on my bedroom ceiling and listening to Cypris Hill. Another night, we took a few hits again; and one friend drove the other two of us around the city. We lay in the back of her pickup truck and watched the sky the entire time. It looked as if we were driving around the set of Beetle juice. Another night, we put the acid in our juice and drank it. I'm not sure how much. Enough to make the floors move like waves in the ocean and walls to drip rainbows down them. I wish I could have painted a picture of some of the visions I saw, but I was not an artist of paintbrushes and canvas but one of pen and paper.

I found one thing I could get lost in, writing. I have always had a passion for putting a pen to paper in such a fashion that the words speak out. I started keeping journals at a young age. My therapists advised me to. My writing came from my soul. I wrote down my deepest emotions, and it was so dark, but it felt so good to get it out of my mind and onto the paper. I'm going to share one of the poems I wrote just to give you an example of the dark place my mind lived in. This one is dated September 1989.

I live my life day by day, it hurts me
I'm being cut up inside
My heart is being ripped apart
I'm feeling so empty inside
My nightmare returns
It echoes in my head
It echoes in my soul
It pulses in my heart

Death is in my hands
It feels so good, it feels so bad
I'm spinning, spinning, spinning away
Nothing is clear, it's hazy red
I'm dying, slowly fading away
My pain is gone.

Even though I kept journals for years, I never wrote about my secret. I eluded to it. I wrote about how it made me feel but never told. I fell in love with putting a pen to paper. It was a release of the chaos in my head to an extent. I have hundreds of these painful emotions that I put on paper over the years, kept in journals, bound tight for only my eyes to see. The writing saved me so many times and in so many ways. In high school, I was in honors English classes. I loved the challenge. When I went on to college, I was able to test out of two required English courses on a national level. Schoolwork in general was easy for me. I obtained good grades somewhat effortlessly. When it came to writing, it was like someone gave me a gift that just kept on giving. When I started reading back through my journals, I began to notice two different, sometimes three different handwriting styles and entries I could not recall making. By this point in my life, it was already normal for me to lose time and do things I couldn't remember doing.

When I wasn't busying myself with lessons, writing, or schoolwork, I found an escape in physical labor. I started working at twelve years of age. My mom presented me with the opportunity to earn money during the summertime, at which I jumped. It would get me out of that godforsaken house during the summer. I didn't care what kind of work it was. My first legitimate job was corn detasseling. It was hard work, but one of the requirements was to go live with my aunt and uncle for the summer an hour away. I didn't care how hard the work was. I was out of that house. I worked that summer job for three summers until I could get my workers permit and get a job close to home. That is exactly what I did. As soon as I turned fifteen, I applied for a workers permit. Because I had excellent grades in school, I obtained it easily and found myself a job at local nursing home as a dietary aide. Working helped me escape, not only from my home situation, but from my own mind.

I saved the best for last. The tool that has saved my lifetime and again. One I have used for the last thirty years of my life. Counseling, yes, I have been in counseling for thirty years; and I won't lie. I still struggle. It didn't start out very smooth. The first counselor I encountered was an absolute *no go*. I had been released from the hospital from a suicide attempt at the age of fourteen and set up a counseling appointment. When I walked in that dimly lit room with big brown leather furniture and there sat a middle aged man, I refused to talk. I told him it was an absolute waste of his time and my parents' money because there was no way in hell I was saying shit to him. That was that. There was no way I was spilling my guts to anyone let alone a man. That was just the beginning of my therapy career. I have been institutionalized at least twenty times in my life, most of the time after I attempted to end the hell I was living in and failed. I was crying for help. I tried to kill myself so many times. I cried out long and hard for someone to help me tell my secret. It wasn't until I was in my twenties that I finally started opening up in therapy sessions and began to start my healing process.

One of my therapists suggested hypnotism to help me recover memories and maybe help with why I was losing time. I absolutely agreed. I needed to know the secrets I had been keeping from myself. If I knew the secrets, maybe I could heal and then maybe I could feel what it felt like to be normal. On the flip side, I'm a little scared because what if knowing is too much for me to handle. The day of my appointment is here. I'm nervous, but I go. I'm sitting in the chair across from my therapist, all ready to be hypnotized. In our last session, he explained what exactly we would be doing; so we get right to business. He's talking in a slow, monotone, rhythmic pattern; and I begin to count backward. When I wake up, I'm on the floor, in the corner of the room, balled up; and I'm crying and saying, "No, Daddy, no. Please, no."

My therapist is crouched down in front of me, talking to me calmly and helping me up to the chair. He wouldn't tell me what had happened. He thought it better to wait until our next session. Before the date for our next session, I received a call from the counseling office. They were explaining to me that I was being assigned a new counselor. I didn't understand what was going on. Needless to say, I never went back. I never found out what happened in that session. I'm unsure why I never returned to find out what had happened. When I requested my medical records from that office to help me write this book, I was told they had been destroyed two weeks prior. I will never know what took place that day.

All the psychiatrists, psychologists, therapists, and counselors I've seen in my lifetime; and there are hundreds have helped me get to where I am today. There is one extraspecial woman who has stuck with me over the last seven years. She hasn't given up on me after all the no-show and late cancelations I've made over the years. She has always had faith in me and my convictions and has given me many healthy tools for my toolbox. Thank you, Char.

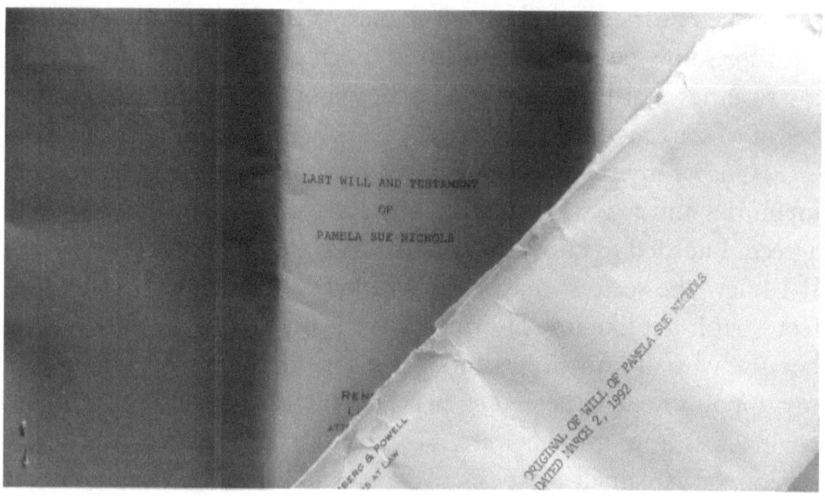

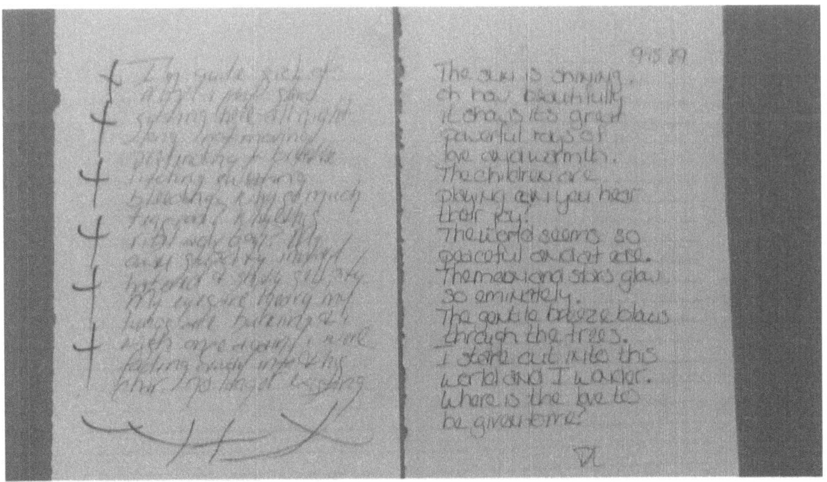
The sun is shining,
oh how beautifully
it shines its great
powerful rays of
love and warmth.
The children are
playing can you hear
their joy.
The world seems so
peaceful and at ease.
The moon and stars glow
so eminently.
The gentle breeze blows
through the trees.
I stare out into this
world and I wonder.
Where is the love to
be given to me?

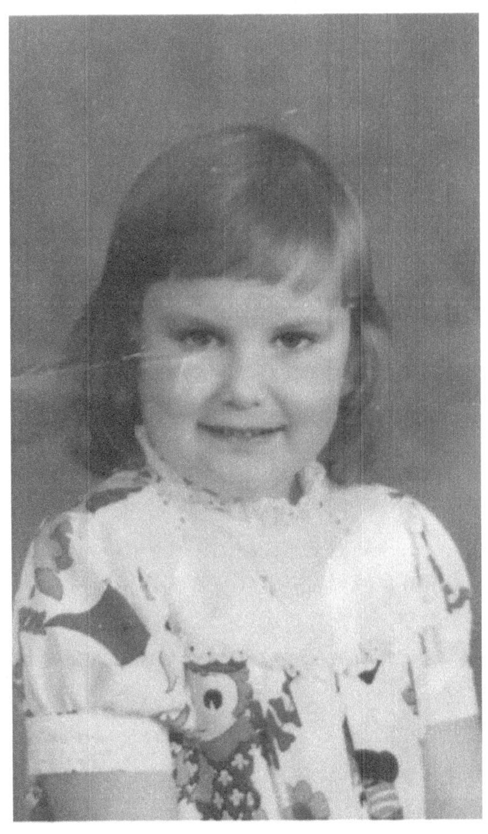

CHAPTER THREE

Recipe for Disaster

I'm sure you must be asking, where is her mom while all this is going on? Why doesn't she see what he's doing to her little girl or better yet stop him. Why on earth is her father doing all these nightmarish things to his innocent, defenseless, little baby girl. These are questions I've asked all my life. In order to get the answers, I had to go back to the beginning. The beginning of my parents' lives. I'm sharing their stories so that you can see how the cycle of abuse is perpetuated. I am in no way making excuses for the travesties committed against me or the oversite of them by my mother, but it is very important that you understand the cycle. There is an old saying "Ignorance is bliss." It is anything but bliss. It is, in all reality, a recipe for disaster. Let me start with the first ingredient, my mom.

I want to be very clear. I absolutely, unequivocally, and unconditionally love my mom. I have had a very hard time coming to terms with many of her decisions because I suffered the consequences for them. They have caused me a lifetime of anguish and pain. There were also times when she saved my life. I know she loved me and she was doing the best with what she had at the time. I can remember her coming into the room. My father would have me pinned in a corner slapping me around. He would get right in my face and backhand me and threaten me. I must have cried out on these occasions because she came and saved me. She would yell at him, "Now that's enough," and he would stop. Why she never just picked me up and just ran away to save me. I'll never really know. She chose to stay. She chose him over me. She chose to stand by her husband and believe his lies. Ultimately, she chose to feed me to the beast. The more I learned about my mother's upbringing and life experiences, the more clear the picture became. Come with me. I'll show you.

What I'm about to share with you about my mother's life is taken from stories she has told me over the years. Her father was raised on a farm and left the home at ten years of age. He did odd jobs and eventually joined the circus to support himself. He was married at a very young age and had a daughter. I'm not sure why that marriage didn't work out. I could speculate, but I won't.

Her mother was raised on a farm and had a daughter from a previous marriage as well. My grandmother's first husband was kicked in the head by a horse and passed away. I don't know the story about how they met and fell in love, but they did and started a life together. My grandmother had her young daughter who had recently suffered the loss of her father, so she needed a dad in her life. My grandfather never told his new wife about the family he had left behind or if he had. The two of them kept it a secret. It took seventy years for that secret to be revealed through genealogy research. My mom was the second addition to their new family, and there would be five more after her. Six girls and two boys. One of the siblings, a baby girl, passed away in infancy due to a condition called spina bifita. They were very poor and raised in a shack with no heat, electric, or running water. This shack I speak of was located on the property on my great-grandparents' home. While my great grandparents were living in a two story, multibedroom home, my grandparents were living with all these children on the same property in the backyard in a shack.

Living on a farm was hard work. The kids went to work with their parents helping with whatever they did to earn money. Chasing chickens down and snapping their necks, beheading them, and plucking their feathers was a common chore as well as collecting eggs, corn detasseling and tending to the animals. Being hired out to do laundry and ironing for the wealthy was one of my grandmother's jobs.

Because there were seven kids, my grandmother made their clothing from what she had available, potato sacks. Yes, she hand-made all the families clothing from the potato sacks after they were done eating the potatoes. Bath time for the children happened one day a week, usually Saturdays to be ready for church on Sunday. They had to haul water from the pump and then warm it over a fire then dump it in a washtub. All the kids took turns in the tub, and they would rotate who went first each week so that they all had an opportunity to be first in the tub and get the clean water once every six weeks.

Their bathroom was an outhouse and toilet paper consisted of old newspapers, magazines, and sometimes old corncobs. Many of their meals consisted of raw potatoes and radish sandwiches. Yes, she was raised very poor at first; but things got better. Eventually, both of my grandparents got better jobs and started building their own home. When I say built their own home, I mean, they dug the foundation, laid the bricks, and the whole nine yards by hand. They were very hard workers. Not only was my grandma a hard worker, she was talented in the kitchen. She made the best home-cooked meals, and her baking was to die for!

My grandfather would go on to own his own shoe repair business that is still open to this day. He coached little league baseball and has a baseball diamond in their hometown named after him. The memories I had of my grandfather were heartwarming ones. He was the *nice guy* when compared to my grandmother, she was the disciplinarian. He always got out the big green blanket and laid it out on the floor for us to play on. He pretended to be a black cat, and I would pretend to be scared. I would try to put rollers in what was left of his hair on his balding head. The first thing he did when I got to their house was put a pizza in the oven for me. He always made a joke about how my grandmother didn't like pizza even though she had never even tried it. I loved to play along and tease my grandma, so I always offered her a piece and tried to get her to try it for the first time.

Oh, the fun we had, watching baseball, eating pizza, and always had a popsicle to finish it up. They were the kind with the ice cream in the middle. I loved my grandpa! He was going to give me his pea green 1973 Chevy Nova when I was old enough to drive. That car was a beauty. It had the front bench style seat, and the apolstry was made of green plaid cloth. That was a great car.

I remember when he started getting real sick with cancer. There was one particular time I went to see him. We were talking. I was about twelve. He said, "Always listen to your grandmother. She can be an honery woman, but she's smart, and she knows what she's talking about." He then stood up and started unbuttoning and unzipping his pants and trying to get me to come over to him. I was like, what is my grandpa doing? He must be going crazy from the cancer. I think I was thirteen when he passed away. I know I attended his funeral, but I have no recollection of it.

It wasn't until about a year ago that I found out my grandpa, the only man I had good memories about, the only man that didn't hurt me as a child, was a pedophile too. I had my suspicions. Allow me to explain. My mom's older sister was diagnosed with Alzheimer's ten years ago. I went to her home to help care for her four days a week. One day, we were sitting at her kitchen table having lunch; and she brought my grandfather up. She said, "He was never my dad, and he was a bad, bad man, a very bad man."

The look of disgust mixed with terror that ensued her face as she spoke those words. I knew then, but I just filed it away. It wasn't until a year ago when my mom was here for a visit, she and I were talking, and out of nowhere, she says, "Your cousin called me today and told me that my dad molested my older sister."

I immediately responded by asking her if he had molested her. She said he had not. My mom went on to say, "She wasn't his real daughter anyway." It took my brain a few moments to digest what she had just said. I told her it did not matter what her relationship was to him. She was a child, and that was horrible.

It was like a light switching on in my brain. It was a missing piece to my puzzle. Although my mom denies being molested. I don't believe her. I believe my grandfather molested several of his children, and here is why. First and foremost, my mom married and stayed with my father. The third child, my mom's sister, married a pedophile and her husband and children molested me. One of my mother's brothers was accused of molesting his stepdaughter. With that being said, let me tell you about my mom and how she met my father.

My mom was a normal teenage girl. She graduated high school. She attended college, first nursing school and then business. Shortly after college, she met her first husband and would stay married to him for fifteen years. She was always a career woman, very independent. She was actually the first female claims adjuster in our city, for which she received an award. Her husband owned his own painting business. They were doing well, for a while at least. She wanted children, and it wasn't coming to fruition. She believed he was unable to give her babies.

He began drinking excessively, hanging out in dive bars, and bringing her home diseases. She became fed up and couldn't continue on in that horrible marriage. She had also met someone to help her get over it. One night, a few weeks after she had left him—upon leaving her job and getting into her car—he chased her down and engaged her in a high speed chase all over the city while he was shooting at her. He had lost his mind. He must have found out that not only did she leave him, she left him for another man. As I mentioned, he owned his own business. Well, it just so happened that the man she met was an employee of her husband. Her husband had brought him around the house one day, and when they met, sparks flew. Prince charming had walked through that door that day and swept her off her feet. He was like her knight in shining armor. She had put up with years of an abusive, childless marriage, full of heartache. He arrived on the seen at a perfect time. This man rescued her. He was handsome, intelligent, funny, and hardworking. A dream come true in her eyes. This man would turn out to be my father.

I cannot tell you stories told to me by my father because he told me very few. What he did tell me was that his mother was crazy and mean and that his parents stole the money he was sending home from the Navy. Both of which turned out to be lies. He was already married when he enlisted in the Navy, and the money was going to his family. We never had conversations. There was no sitting at the kitchen table talking or riding in the car chatting it up. The time I spent alone with my father was strictly reserved for damaging me in any way possible. What I can tell you is a story about my father that he showed me. I can share with you the facts about his life told to me by the family he terrorized before I existed. My father did not tell me stories of his upbringing because he was keeping a secret. I do not know anything about my paternal grandparents, aside from being told, I would have loved my grandmother and that my grandfather was an abusive pedophile. Ingredient number two, my father.

I wish I could be as equally clear about my feelings toward my father as I am my mother, but I cannot be. You see, he twisted my perception by teaching me pain was love. The only time he showed me affection was to get what he wanted out of me sexually; and when that didn't work, it quickly became violent. There were times I felt like I may have loved him, at best I felt sorry for him. I think I may have loved him when I was little, and I didn't know any better; but for the most part, my feelings toward my father were composed of fear, anger, and hate. With that being said, let me tell you about the man who would become my dad.

My father was the eldest of six children. There were three boys and three girls, born and raised in Ohio. My father, one other of his brothers and one of his sisters, from what I can confirm all grew up to be pedophiles like their father. My father graduated high school and went on to get married to his first of three wives at the age of eighteen. They had five children together, three girls and two boys. He was enlisted in the Navy. This was not a voluntary enlistment. He was in trouble for deceptive practices; and in those days, they gave you a choice between serving your country or going to jail. So off to the Navy he went. He was enlisted during the Korean War and was a cook on a ship. He was honorably discharged twice; and the third time, he served he requested an honorable discharge and was denied. He was later dishonorably discharged for misconduct. Upon one of his discharges, his wife and children went to greet him when he was getting off the ship. To their surprise, there was another woman there to meet him; and she was pregnant. I do not know what became of that, but I'm pretty sure I have more siblings than what I am aware of. At one point in his first marriage, he chased his wife and eldest daughter down with a rifle in attempt to take their lives. He was very abusive, not only to his wife but his children as well; and then one day, it all came to a halt.

One afternoon, he was taking a shower; and there was a knock at his door. The police had come to arrest him for deceptive practices. Once he was in custody, his eldest daughter confided in her mother that her father had been molesting her, and it had escalated into rape. To prove she was telling the truth to her mother, she told her where he hid the big knife he would threaten her with if she told on him. When his wife went searching for the knife as instructed by her daughter, she found it. Immediately, she knew her daughter was being truthful. At that time, he was being held in custody before sent off to the Navy again; and she paid him a visit and confronted him. She later filed for divorce, and he would never return to his wife and five children. There were never any charges brought against him.

I am unsure of how he met his second wife. Truthfully, I only know a few things about their relationship. She was a lawyer or legal assistant and had two children from a previous relationship, a girl and a boy. I do not know how long they were married or if they had any children together. What I can tell you is that he held her children hostage in their home, turned the gas oven on, and was threatening to blow them up. I can only imagine the horrific events that led up to this episode. Whether or not he was ever punished for this incident, I don't know. What I do know is that after this incident, he moved to Illinois, found a job as a painter, and met my mom.

When they first started their life together, they didn't have a lot of money, as my father gave up his job to be with my mom. They lived in a small, upper apartment across from a cemetery. They were married in January 1972. He invited his children to their wedding, but they did not come. By sending out that invitation, his oldest daughter seized the moment and asked to come visit. She had to warn his new wife of his past. She had to stop him from hurting any more children the way he had hurt her. I wasn't even thought into existence yet when my sister visited her father and new wife. She came with a desperate warning for my mother, "Don't stay with this man. He is a monster." My sister told her that her new husband was a child abuser and molester. Because this was her husband, she shared these accusations with him. His reply was simply that she was jealous and wanted to see him back with her mother. She was just making up stories to break them up he told my mom, and she believed him with no questions asked. My sister returned home to her family in Michigan. It wasn't long before my mom became pregnant with me, and I was born. Guess what, my sister came back for me. She came and helped take care of me and tried to protect me. I'm not sure how long she stayed or what the circumstances were for her departure, but it doesn't matter. The fact that she came and that she tried means the world to me. That was the first example of love I was ever shown. It would be over forty years before I would learn of her love for me.

Now that I have shown you, given you a glimpse into my parents upbringing and lives before me, you can clearly see how the merging of their lives were a perfect recipe for my disaster. There is one more very important thing I must share with you before we continue making this journey through my life. Someone came into my life that would change it forever. She would be the first person I cared for and loved, my little sister.

CHAPTER FOUR

The First Love of My Life

I begged, pleaded, and prayed for a little sister for a few years. I was so alone. I wanted so badly to have someone to play with, someone to share my toys with. I wanted a little sister to share my room with and make forts and tents with. I needed someone to run through the sprinkler with in the summer and make snowmen in the snow in the winter. I wanted a Minnie me that I could carry around, hug, and give all my love too. I prayed every night for God to give me a little sister. I would pray and tell God I promised to be the best girl and the best big sister in the whole wide world if he would just give me little sister. My mom and dad tried having another baby, but my mom had a miscarriage and few years later a hysterectomy, but that didn't stop me from asking for a miracle. One day, God answered my prayers. My mom came to me and told me I was going to have a sister. My parents had signed up to be foster parents.

I am getting a sister? Oh my goodness! I couldn't contain my happiness! The best day of my life was about to happen! I'm jumping up and down, clapping my hands, yay, yay, yay! How old is she? What does she look like? I can't wait to hug her and cuddle her and love her. When will she be here? What is her story? Why is she in foster care? I wanted to know everything about her so I could know her so she felt comfortable in her new home. It's hard to put into words the excitement I felt. The anticipation was one hundred times more than that of a trip to Disney World!

I'm going to share with you my sister's story from my eyes. This is not her story in its entirety. It is just a brief excerpt, as I hope one day, she will be inspired to share her story on her journey through her healing process. My sister was born in April of 1979. Her birth parents were young when they brought her into this world although they loved her very much. They were incapable of caring for a baby. Unfortunately, her birth father made some poor decisions and landed himself in jail leaving a young single mother to care for her daughter on her own. She tried with the help of her family, but it was just too hard and something just wasn't right. There were reports of my sister being put in baths of extremely hot water and scrubbed raw when being bathed by her mom. She was at one point found malnourished as a result of being left at home unattended for days on end. To survive, she was eating whatever she could find and drinking water from the toilet. At this point, she was taken from her mother and placed into the foster care system. She was only two and a half. At first her birth mom's family took my sister into their care. Her great grandmother and grandmother tried to care for her, but she was too much for them to handle as they were getting up in age. I was told stories of how my sister would chase them around the house with a yard stick, and they would have to run and lock themselves in rooms. After living a short time with her grandmother's, she was then moved with her aunt, her mother's sister. It would only be few months that stay would last, and her aunt contacted the foster care social worker and requested they find my sister a foster family. That is when they contacted my parents to let them know they had a beautiful baby girl who needed their care. She was three years old.

I was nine years old when I received the best gift I've ever been given, my baby sister. My mom sat me down and explained to me the things that my new little sister had been through already in life. She explained to me I that I needed to be patient with her and give her lots of love. She told me I was going to be her big sister now, and I needed to watch out for her. We got bunk beds for my room, now it would be our room. Yes! My mom bought her clothes, and I made room in our dresser and closet. It was really happening. He heard me. God really heard, listened, and answered my prayers.

The day is here. My little sister is coming to her new home today to meet her new family. Man, I am so excited! I was ready. I have the toy room all clean with a few toys out I can play with her. Our room is all clean and beds made. I am all showered and presentable, ready, ready, ready! There it is, the knock on the door! She is finally here!

In came the social worker with my new little sister hand in hand. She was so small and absolutely adorable. I went over to her and bent down and said, "Hi, I'm your new sister. My name is Pam."

I can remember how frightened she was, and how much I wanted to make her feel comfortable. Eventually, she left the social worker's side and came with me, her new big sister; and I showed her our room and all around the house. We went downstairs and played in the toy room. I offered my new little sister any and all my toys to play with. It was then I realized, we would have to get her some new toys because most of mine were not age appropriate for a three-year-old. Mom called us for dinner. Us, yes, it was us now, not just me. As we sat at the dinner table, I told mom we would need to go toy shopping for my new little sister; and she agreed. We would go tomorrow.

It was time for bed. We went in and got our pajamas on. I tried to tell Sylvia. She should sleep on the bottom bunk so she wouldn't fall off, but she insisted on being up on the top bunk. I learned the very first night, my new little sister was brave and independent. I mean, what three-year-old wants to sleep on the top bunk all alone? My sister is the answer. I helped her up the ladder and tucked her all in then I got in bed.

At some point, during the night, I heard big *thud*! It was Sylvia. She fell off the top bunk in her sleep. I jumped up, scooped her up in my arms, and put her in bed with me. I held her in my arms until we both fell asleep. I took care of her like my mommy told me too. Not too long after we fell asleep. I was woken up by being kicked. Sylvia was a mover and shaker in her sleep. I did not get much sleep, and that would be the first night in my career of caring for my sister though the middle of the night. At three years old, she already had night terrors. She would kick and fight in her sleep, and that wasn't all she would sleepwalk as well. We shared a room, and my parents were asleep; so I just took care of her. I woke her and comforted her when she was kicking and fighting in her sleep. I would calm her down and rub her arm or her back to help her back to sleep. When I realized she wasn't in bed anymore, I would go find her in the house and coax her back to bed.

One night, after we had moved to the new house. She was sleep-walking. She got out of the house and went over to the neighbor's house wearing only her underwear, wrapped in her blanket. She rang the doorbell and said she needed help because the house was on fire. Now, I do know that she was involved in a house or apartment fire when she was with her biological mother. I do not know all the details. Her sleepwalking and night terrors were her acting out what had happened to her. I took care of her just like my mommy said to. I was my sister's keeper. I just wanted to give her all the love in the world and make her feel safe, feel safe like I neither one of us ever had. I would spend the rest of my childhood and the beginning of my adulthood trying to protect my little sister. It makes me absolutely sick to say that, but it is the truth. Even though I know it was in no way my fault for bringing my sister into my father's house of terror, I've lived with guilt all of my adult life. Not only did I have my little sister to protect from this monster of a man, we had a pet. Precious was our little, white, female Maltese; and my dad was as mean to that dog as he was to us kids. I was always getting in the way of him kicking or hitting the dog. He was always making her yelp, and I would run into the room to see what was happening to her just like I did with my sister.

We were like all siblings. We played. We fought. We got into trouble; but you see, getting into trouble in our house was a bit different than the average home. My sister and I didn't get time-outs or even spankings. We got bloody noses, fat lips, choked, kicked, and punched. I tried to save her from him as much as I could. I really, really tried; but I was just a little girl too. I would jump in front of her to take the blows only to be tossed aside like a rag doll or kicked out of the way like the dog. If my mom was home, I would yell for her; and she would come stop him sometimes. If she wasn't home, that was a totally different story; and I was powerless to save her, but

I tried. If you know what it is like to see and hear someone you love being tortured, and there isn't a thing you can do to stop it from happening, then you know our pain. If you haven't had that experience in life then I can only tell you that is the equivalent of being in hell. We were so small, and he was so big and angry. There were times when my sister and I would be fighting over some little kid stuff, and I would tell on her, and it is those times I feel most guilty for because it was my fault he hurt her, and I was supposed to be protecting her.

I was about ten when I got the exciting news. My dad was remodeling the attic so my sister and I could have our own rooms. It was a big attic, and I had big plans for it. I even helped Sylvia figure out how she would arrange her new room. I explained how she was a getting to be a big girl so she could have a big-girl room! Because my little sister was such an independent soul, she happily agreed with me. She did not spend very many nights in her big-girl room. She always came up and got in bed with me. I believe this is when my father started molesting my sister. I believe our rooms were separated so that he could do to her, what he had done to me. I can't prove it because I can't remember a lot of my childhood. There are huge gaping holes in my memory, like black holes that sucked my memories into them.

I would love to tell you specifics of all the time we spent playing together or the details of the family vacations we went on, but it is difficult to do so. What I do know is that there wasn't actually family interaction. It was me and my sister. I don't know if we confided in each other about the abuse. I simply cannot recall. The brutal tactics our father used not only caused me to disassociate, but my sister as well. Disassociation didn't just serve its purpose as a survival tool for us to get through the abuse our father dealt out. It robbed us of many, many good memories we had together. I will share what I am able to.

My sister has always been a fighter but not by choice but because she has always had to fight. She had to fight for her life, her first three years in this life, and then fight my father the rest of her life. He taught her how to fight, literally. I remember this little boy was picking on her at day care, and he just wouldn't stop, so my dad taught her how to fight. The next time that kid picked on her, my sister fought back and punched him. Yes, my little sister was a firecracker and wasn't going to take crap from anyone. She wasn't just tough with her fists. She had a mouth on her of a sailor. Now I had heard all these *naughty words* from many adults around me, but coming from the mouth of my three-year-old sister was a shocker! You name it. She said it. Fuck, shit, damn, cock sucker, and the list goes on and on. She was a product of her environment. She was only repeating what she had heard. My mom would correct her and sometimes put her in time-out. I remember times when she would let one fly; and our father's response was smacking her in the mouth, putting hot sauce on her tongue, or making her put soap in her mouth. Please remember I tried in every way possible to protect my baby sister, but there were somethings that were being done that I didn't realize were wrong. I didn't know to save her because I had been subjected to the same things, and I thought they were normal behaviors. I thought all dads smacked their children around to keep them in line, scared the living shit out of them with threats to their lives, and molested them.

Now the social worker came and made regular home visits. She would talk to me and my parents and even to my sister alone. We never told our secret. At the age of six, my parents legally adopted Sylvia. We went to court that morning. I can remember sitting in the big wooden benches. We were all dressed up. This was a big important day. It was going to be official. Of course, Sylvia was my sister; but now, it was really real; and no one could come and take her away. It was always my fear that her birth parents would decide they wanted her back. I believe this was a fear was emulated by our mother, nonetheless, it had become mine as well. Our parents threw my sister an adoption party with family and friends. We had food and cake, and they presented her with a gift with an engraving that included her adoption date on it. That is one thing I can say was done correctly and with love by our parents.

My mom's way of dealing with our home situation was to get my sister away from it as much as possible as she had done with me when I as little—lesson, lesson, lessons. Dance lessons, tumbling lessons, swimming lessons, whatever lessons were available my sister took them. It kept her away from home, away from torture. School all day, lessons all night. In going to all these lessons, my sister found her love for the art of dance and excelled. As writing was my escape, my love, my passion, dance was hers. My parents even installed mirrored sliding doors on her closet so that she could practice in her room. Yes, dance was her love; and she was an amazing performer. I loved watching her dance, seeing the freedom she felt, watching her spirit soar.

During the summer, my sister went to camp. She attended camp five days a week for the entire summer; and one night, a week they had a sleep over there. She loved that camp. She never wanted to leave, and she was always eager to go back. It was an escape for her, a happy place that took the harsh reality of home away for little while. Oh, the fun she had there.

Wednesday night was family night. Mom, dad, and I all got in the car to head out to camp to see what my sister had learned. We usually stopped on the way and got Kentucky Fried chicken because Sylvia loved it. We sat at picnic tables and had dinner before heading into the woods to be entertained by the songs and skits the campers had been practicing. She was so proud to be up there performing. She absolutely loved it, and I was proud of her. These camp songs she learned over those summers would become some of the good memories we were able to hold on to, and we would sing them together for years. We would sing them in the van on our road trips to Disney World, in the car on our way to our grandparents' house, in our rooms while were playing. One of our favorites was the infamous Miss Marry Mac, the game were you sing and make up hand claps together along with Agalina Magdalina. Those songs, as simple and amusing as they were, meant so much more to me than the words they contained. They symbolized happiness and a bonding with my little sister. One we were able to hold on to.

Speaking of bonding, it reminds me of a story, one that got my baby sister expelled from church school in her elementary years. It was all my fault. I'm not sure of our ages; but one day, my neighborhood friend and I were playing in the woods on our property just across the creek. We had decided to be blood sisters. Yes, blood sisters. We had found a sharp object, and we're going to each cut our hands and rub them together to become blood sisters. Just as I began to cut my hand, up through the trees comes Sylvia. We swore her to secrecy and continued our ritual right in front of her. Well, she went to school; and while on recess one day, she was caught repeating the ritual with a school mate that she had learned from me. I taught my little sister many useful things along the way: how to run, how to hide, how to try to stay out of trouble, and how to play cards. Yes, indeed, she loved playing cards; and let me tell you, all the card games I taught her, she kicked my butt in every single one. She has a competitive spirit and has always loved a challenge. There is one thing I didn't teach her that she learned on her own, how to tell.

I was eighteen and had recently moved out of the house into my own place when I received a call from my mom. What she said to me would rock my world and send me into a frenzy. She asked me if I believed my sister was telling the truth when she was saying our dad was molesting her. My sister had broken the silence and confided in a family friend, who in turn told my mom. I lost my mind. I told my mom you get her away from him now. Today, figure it out, or I was going to call the cops and social services and get custody of her myself if she didn't listen to me. I swore to her I was going to call the police and have our father locked up if she didn't act fast. I told her she wasn't even to let him around her. Don't take her home tonight. Don't take her home until you have a new one to take her too without that monster in it. And guess what? She listened. She believed me, and she acted. She got a townhouse and moved out. She got my sister away. I did what my mom herself had instructed me to do. I protected my baby sister. I may have failed to be able to so many times before but not this time. I put a stop to that monster. My sister was twelve. It would be a year of them living on their own before my mom would return home with my sister. In the meantime, I had taught her so much more.

One night, when she was about thirteen, my friend and I were going to see Jurassic park at the movie theater. It had just come out, and she was begging to come with. I gave in, and my mom finally agreed to let her go. When we got to the movie theater parking lot, I parked the car and proceeded to pack a bowl with marijuana. I asked her if she wanted to try it, and I taught her how to smoke weed. I got my little sister high for the first time. So high we couldn't even remember the movie we had just watched. Yes, I taught my sister many things, directly and indirectly as she watched my actions growing up. I taught her to lie to stay out of trouble, how to sneak out of the house, and to ask my mom for birth control when she was ready to have sex so she wouldn't get pregnant, like her sister.

As she got older, I started hanging out with her. She took me to parties with her and introduced me to her friends. As time went by, some of her friends became my friends. She always made me feel included and loved. One night, she asked me to accompany her on a date. She wanted me to meet this new guy. You know, get my sister stamp of approval. We met him at a local bar, and we're having drinks and shooting pool. He was a pretty cool guy. As the night progressed, we became quite tipsy; and it was time to go. Thank god there was a McDonald's across the parking lot because these two chicks needed nourishment. Only the drive through was open, so we hopped in her new man's car. As we started driving across the parking lot, my sister started feeling sick. He pulls the car over in front of the McDonald's parallel to a very busy street at a very busy time of the night. My sister gets out because she's going to toss her cookies, and I get out to hold her hair. While she is throwing up all over the curb, I decide I have to pee; and it can't wait. I pull down my pants, lean, and squat against the car and let it loose. I'm trying to stay clear of her puke, and she's trying to steer clear of my urine hitting the ground at g-force speed. After we are all done with that spectacular display of grace and beauty, we get back in the car with this poor unsuspecting guy. We are laughing and apologizing. I'm sure we smelled just great.

He was a perfect gentleman with the situation. He drove us to my house and made sure we got in okay. I'm sure that is a story he will tell the rest of his life, as will my sister and I. I held my sister's hair back while she puked, got her water and bread; and I eventually made her a bed in the bathroom by the toilet after I knew she okay. This was not our only drunken night together, but one of the most memorable. My sister and I got matching tattoos on our arms. They are cherry blossoms with the Japanese conji for elder and younger sister. She is my heart and soul, the first love of my life, my ride or die; and I would do absolutely anything for her including giving my life to save hers. It is true that many of our memories were stolen from us, and we do not share the same birth parents. Despite all that, we still have an inseparable bond, one that only sisters are capable of having.

CHAPTER FIVE

Life After

At the young age of seventeen, I became pregnant; and at eighteen gave birth to my first beautiful baby girl. I must explain the years leading up to conceiving my first and then we will continue our journey into my life after the abuse stopped. The sexual abuse had stopped. I'm not sure of the exact age to be honest with you. I believe it was around the time my sister came into the home or that year after when our rooms were separated. He stopped sexually abusing me because he had my sister to do it to now. It's very hard for me to put into words the feelings and emotions that are attached to that statement. I stated previously that I know it wasn't really my fault, but that is hard to come to terms with. It is a guilt I have carried most of my life. Although the sexual abuse had stopped, the physical, verbal, and emotional abuse continued.

Today, my mom and I are baking a cake for my birthday. I love baking with my mom. My favorite part is licking the spoon and the bowl clean. We measured everything. I mixed it up like my mom taught me. She poured it in the pan and put it in the oven. Now it's time for the best part. I'm standing in the kitchen with the plastic green mixing bowl in one hand, and the spatial coated with chocolate in the other. Just as I am getting ready to take my first lick, my dad comes up from the basement and said, "You really don't need that now do you. You are already too fat. Leave it alone and wash it up." I am ten years old. Those words and variations of them hurt me every time they were delivered, and they were on a frequent basis. As I became older, the assaults on my self-esteem did not cease. I became a hussy, a whore, and a prostitute when I tried looking nice. Not only were the kids at school teasing me and calling me names, so was my father. The price I paid to protect myself was a costly one. I had always taken pride in my studies but it came to a point where it was starting to have an effect on my schoolwork.

In between report cards were the progress reports. They were mailed home as well as the report cards. Today is the day all the teachers let us students know our midterm grades so that we can see what improvements need to be made if any. All my classes are good so far, A's and B's. I arrive at my seventh hour and am seated for class to begin. The teacher gives us an assignment to work on while he is reviewing our grades with us individually. My turn. So far so good, so I'm confident I'm doing well. When my teacher reveals to me I have a C in his class, no! It can't be true. I can feel the blood rushing to my face, and the tears swelling up in my eyes. I'm going to be killed when get home. That's it. My life is over, and it's going to be painful. I frantically ask the teacher if there is anything I can do to fix it before they are mailed out. He tells me no. There isn't. They are already mailed. I can't keep the tears back any longer, and I burst into tears right in front of the teacher and the entire seventh grade class. He escorts me out to the hallway to find out what's wrong. I explain to him that if my dad sees this grade he will kill me. "You don't understand. I'm serious." I'm pleading please, please, please.

He doesn't believe me. He doesn't understand. "You can get it up before the final grade comes out. You just missed a couple of assignments. I'm sure you are over exaggerating," he said to me; but he doesn't know the rules in my house. I'm not allowed to get any grades lower than a B, or else, I can't go home. My mom gets home after my dad, and she won't be there to save me. I don't know what to do. I don't have a choice. I just have to go and face the music. I'm dying inside.

When I get home, I go straight to my room and lock both doors. In this house, my room is in the basement. One of my bedroom doors is at the bottom of the stairs, the other is on the other side of the room and leads to a hallway. I leave my coat on in case I can get away and run out the back door. I crouch all the way in the corner of my bed and the wall and pull the covers over me, and I wait. I wait like I've waited so many other times when I knew the punishment was coming, and I pray. I pray for my life like all the other times. *Please, Jesus. Please, God, just let him die on his way home from work. Send a big truck to smash into him. Do anything. Just stop him from hurting me, please, please, please. I'm begging you.* My prayers go unheard once again. I heard the garage door close. The door to the house close. I heard my dad walking in the kitchen, and he stops. He must be looking at the mail. "Get ready," I tell myself; and here he comes, stomping across the floor toward the stairs and then down the stairs. He comes so hard and fast. It sounds like rolling thunder. He turns the knob, and it's locked. I have no choice but to get little. I crouch as small as I can into the corner and cover up and recite in my head get little, get little, get little when, *bam!* The bedroom door flies open and hits the wall. He kicked the door open, and he comes flying across the room toward me; and poof, just like that. I'm gone.

Suzzie saved me again. I wasn't even sure if she was still here. I am thirteen years old. I have to share with you when Suzzie comes and I lose time. Sometimes it's just for the duration of the actual abuse, and sometimes it's for days, weeks, and sometimes months.

After that, I made sure I kept my grades up that was for sure. It wasn't long before I was granted my worker's permit. I could be away from home most of the time. One of my teachers at school was organizing an educational trip to Europe, and I had my mind set to go on it. I worked my rear end off to save the money to go. I would be gone for an entire month, away from all my problems and far away at that. I wasn't going to miss this for anything. I worked extra and saved, and I took my butt on that trip. It was one of the best times of my life. It was in Rome, Italy on a beach. That I would experience my first kiss, real kiss.

He was an Italian guy that didn't speak English, but verbal language means nothing when chemistry takes over. We were on a beach at night lying in the sand. You could hear the ocean waves in the background. What could be more romantic? He was trying to do more, but my friend convinced me to come back to the hotel as it was getting late. If it weren't for her, who knows what would have happened. I made it back to the hotel just in the nick of time, they were closing and locking the doors for the night. I've been inside the Roman coliseum, to the top of the Eiffel Tower, seen the leaning tower of pizza, walked the open markets and the streets or morocco, and so much more. Although we were only sixteen, we sat at the bars and ate fish and chips and drank beer. There was no age limit to drink alcohol in many of the European countries we toured, and I took full advantage of it. Not only was I halfway around the world, but I could get drunk as well. There couldn't be a further escape from my problems as this. I drank too much too frequently on that trip, but I had the time of my life! When I returned home, I was saddened to find out my bird had died. At the age of nine, I was bribed to stop sucking my thumb with a yellow canary. His name was PJ, and he sang and sang all the time. I loved that bird. I made my parents take me and that bird to Chicago to a bird specialist when he got sick. I cleaned his cage, gave him his medications, and talked to him all the time. His singing calmed my soul. Now he's dead, and please know I believe my father killed that bird the day I left on that trip. I'm sure he was smart enough to do it after my mom fell asleep and left it there for her to find in the morning because that's just the kind of guy hc was.

One evening, upon arriving to my job as a dietary aide, I am pulled aside by the owners and informed I am being terminated. "Why?" I asked. "What's going on?" I had called in sick the night before, but I don't do it all the time. I don't understand. As the owner explains to me how someone saw me at high school football game the night I called in, I couldn't believe my ears. I absolutely was not at that football game. There was no way. I explained. I was at home. My boss replies by telling me this person not only saw me at that game, but spoke to me as well. There is no way that happened. Someone is trying to get me fired. Who was is it. I want to know. I called in because I had cut my arms up so bad I wasn't able to hide it at work. So I lied to my boss and told him I had got caught in some rose bushes helping my dad cut them down. He asked me to prove it.

When I pull up my sleeves and show him my arms, he replied, "That doesn't look like that's what happened, and I don't believe you weren't at that game. I have no choice but to fire you."

I am devastated. How will I explain this to my parents? My dad is going to kill me. Now I don't remember being at that foot-ball game. I was accused of being at that game Friday night. I had fallen asleep after I had called of work that day, but that doesn't mean Suzzie didn't go to that game.

I was already in a dark place and had cut extensively on both of my arms; and now, I had lost my job over something I didn't even do. My solution was to cut myself even more, so I cut on myself with a razor blade until I fell asleep that night. When I woke up the next morning, I washed up my wounds and got dressed, making sure I wore long sleeves. I went and found my mom and told her that I needed to go to the hospital when she asked why I told her I was feeling suicidal. She and my father took me. As I sat in the room with the social worker, I was afraid to show her my arms; but I knew I had to. I didn't show my parents they didn't know. I told the social worker I had something to show her, but I didn't want anyone to be mad at me. I know I need help because I can't stop doing this, and I pulled up my sleeves to show her. I had sliced both my forearms up to the point that you couldn't really see skin. There were hundreds of razor blade slices, some were scabbed up and some were fresh. She tried to keep her composure but couldn't and excused herself, and it wasn't long before a psychiatrist entered the room. He asked me a bunch of questions after asking to see my arms; and when he was done, he asked me if I had any questions. I said, "I have one question. Am I staying?"

When he told me that I was, I was scared but more than any-thing I felt relieved. This was my first admission to a psychiatric hos-pital. I would remain there for six weeks. It wasn't so bad in there. I made friends especially with this one boy. He was there because he told his dad he worshiped satan. Silly kid, I think he just wanted attention or a break from his house. Nevertheless, we became good friends. We had something in common. No one understood us.

Even when I was in a safe place and receiving counseling daily, I never told my secret. I didn't tell because that would make it real and I would have to face it. What I did tell them is that I had a little girl living in my head, and she talked to me. I told them about Suzzie, not the purpose she served, only that she existed. Upon revealing my secret, I was placed on antidepressants and antipsychotics and was recommended to be sent to a long term hospital for nine more months of care. Of course, my parents refused and I'm sure my father was worried every time I went in to the hospital that I would squeal on him. Maybe if my parents would have agreed to let me go, I would have gotten the help I needed but they didn't and the vicious cycle continued on.

After I was discharged from the hospital, I returned to my normal home life. I went back to school, and I found another job as a dietary aide at another local nursing home. I also kept in touch with some of the friends I made in the hospital especially the boy who worshiped satan. We talked for a while over the phone and then set up a date. I picked him up, and we went to the movies. This was my first date. I couldn't believe it. A guy thought I was pretty and wanted me to be his girlfriend. As we sat and watched the movie, we were holding hands; and I was thinking about what I could do to make him happy. You know, keep him around. I remembered how I was trained. Putting a man's penis in my mouth makes him happy, so that's exactly what I did, and that's exactly what it did. We dated for about six months when I realized if I wanted to keep my man around, I needed to go all the way with him. When someone is sexually abused as a child, it has many long-term effects, one of which is on their sexuality. It can go from one extreme to another some victims abstain from sex on all levels and want nothing to do with it. Others become sexually charged and extremely promiscuous. In my case, it was the later of the two.

It was the summer of 1989, my parents were planning a trip to Wisconsin where were had a trailer on a resort. We went on vacation here multiple times a year. I asked if my boyfriend could come with us this time; and to my surprise, they agreed. Our trailer was a single wide, but my father had built a screened in porch that ran the length of the trailer. It wasn't uncommon for us to sleep out there, and so my boyfriend and I made beds on the lounge chairs. The fire was still going out in the fire pit, so we took a blanket and laid out by the fire. We were just talking about teenage stuff when I suggested we play a game. It went like this. On the count of three, we both say what we are thinking. This was a similar game my father taught me when I was a little girl, except when we counted to three he would make me touch him on his private areas. I counted. One, two, three and then blurted out, fuck me. He was shocked but hastily replied okay. We moved the blanket over to the next trailer lot that was vacant. I was nervous and scared; but I knew if I wanted to keep him, I had to do this. It hurt me, but I was used to pain. I pretended it didn't; but the whole time, all I could think was just let him hurry up and get it over with like I did with my dad. I'm sixteen years old.

Once I started having sex, it was like a drug; and I couldn't get enough. I was only with one person, but we had sex everywhere: in cars, up against trees, all over my parents' house for the next year. I also associated sex as being love because that was what I was taught growing up. I was so in love with this boy, and no one could tell me anything different. I even let him give me a matching cross tattoo on my left hand, the homemade kind made with a pencil, needle, thread, and India ink. I'm sure it was painful, but I don't recall. I was also taught that love was painful. I was only loveable if I was sexually pleasing a man. Because love was pain, I picked a partner who was guaranteed to hurt me. He was always cheating on me with other girls including my best friend. I decided this world would be better off without me. I can't stop cutting myself. It's the only thing that takes away the madness in my head.

I do not remember much about this suicide attempt, only that I was admitted to the psychiatric hospital for a few weeks. I believe Suzzie had a hand in this one. Honestly, I am unsure if I make the suicide attempts and Suzzie takes over, or if Suzzie takes over and makes the attempts herself, or if there is someone else up there that wants me dead. Everything gets blurred. I remember some things but not others. This is my third suicide attempt and fourth hospitalization. I am seventeen years old.

It would not be long after the last suicide attempt that I would attempt to take my life again. My first and second stays at the psychiatric hospital gave me the ammunition I needed to get the job done. I have all kinds of pills, definitely enough to put me under for good. I retrieve the pills from the kitchen cupboard and pour myself a drink. I open both bottles and pour out a handful. I put them in my mouth and follow up by washing them down. I do this until both bottles are gone, and I go lie down in my bed. When my mom came home, she came into my room to check on me; and I am talking funny, slurring my words. She asks me if I did something wrong, and I tell her I took all the pills. She puts me in the car and off to the emergency room we go. I'm hooked up to all kinds of monitors, and they are drawing blood. They give me something to make me throw up. After a while, a doctor comes in and told me one of the tests they took came back positive. I am pregnant. I am seventeen years old.

I wasn't upset that I was pregnant. I was happy. It gave me a reason to live. When my mom asked me about having an abortion, I was appalled to say the least. This is my baby, and no one is going to take that from me. I'm going to be a mommy. I'm going to be a mommy. I'm going to be a mommy! Well, that's it. I have to take care of myself for my baby, and I'm going to do exactly that. They did an ultrasound, and I am only a couple of weeks along; but that little dot, that little blurb is my baby. I'm going to love it more than the world. I'm due at the end of May. So much to do, so much to plan for. I'm going to give my baby all my love and so much more.

After the emergency room visit, I was admitted to an inpatient psychiatric hospital and stayed for four weeks. Upon my release, I returned home. I returned to school and to work. I had been trying to get a hold of my boyfriend, the father of my baby, and was unable to. My mom informed me that she had contacted his parents and told them about the baby. As a result, he was kicked out of his father's house and was living with his mom. I had no idea how to find him. I figured it out though and tracked him down. His mom was excited. She actually helped me pick out baby names. My boyfriend did not share the same feelings. He wasn't around through my pregnancy, didn't want anything to do with me or our baby. It was perfectly okay by me. My friends and my mom supported me. That's all I needed.

As I mentioned earlier, I attended a private Christian school. I had to go to the school and inform them I was pregnant. When I did tell my school, they informed me when I started showing I would have to quit coming to school and be homeschooled for the rest of my pregnancy. When I returned to school after my month long stay in a psych ward, everyone looked at me when I would walk by and whisper to each other. I went from being the fat kid in class to the crazy pregnant girl. There had only been one other pregnant girl in our school, and she had an abortion and was allowed to come back to school. Our school taught abortion was a sin, so I had a hard time wrapping my mind around the fact that I was getting kicked out for keeping my baby. Little did I know, everything would work out; and this would be my first lesson in how everything happens for a reason.

I straightened myself up. I kept up with my schoolwork. I went to work as scheduled, kept all my doctor's appointments; and I stopped cutting myself. I made sure I kept my mind right even though the father of my child to be was missing in action, and I was facing this all alone. One day, when I was about five months along, I started having cramping. This wasn't good, not good at all. I told my mom, and we went to the hospital. I couldn't lose this baby. I had already fought so hard just to keep it. I was admitted to the hospital for preterm labor and given medicine to stop the labor.

I spent a week lying in that hospital bed. I was sent home on bed rest, but that didn't happen. I had a life to live, school, work, and chores at home. When I was discharged, I went about life as normal. I made sure I took time every day to read out loud to my baby. I played soothing music through earphones, which I had placed on my belly. I wanted my baby to feel loved before it even got here. I didn't have the perfect love story for bringing a baby into this world, but I didn't care. I knew I could give my baby enough love. I had to make plans for my delivery; and because the dad wasn't around, I asked my neighbor to help me deliver. She had coached many women through their deliveries, so she knew what she was doing, and I trusted her. She was like a second mom to me. She agreed to help me, and I was so grateful. We were even going to go to Lamaze classes together. It would be because of her influence that I would go on to help multiple young mothers bring their babies into this world.

Aside from the preterm labor, everything was going smoothly with my pregnancy until I was about six months along when I noticed my feet swelling. I asked the doctor at my next appointment about it. I was given a list of foods to eat that would help get the water off my body. *Natural diuretics* it was labeled. We went to the store and got most of the things on the list. I ate according to the list. I cut out salt and salty foods. Even though I was instructed by my doctor to strict bed rest, I was out mowing a quarter acre of yard with a push mower as instructed by my father. None of my shoes fit anymore. I had resorted to wearing slippers in size 10 when my normal shoe size was a 7. At my next doctor's appointment, I was given the same advice; but I was to be on bed rest for real now. My school made me leave and gave me a home tutor. My coach for delivery came over, and we practiced Lamaze together in my living room. Bed rest wasn't going to stop me.

I must explain that at my Obstetricians office, I had a primary doctor; but they rotated me with all the doctors so that I would be comfortable with whoever was on-call for my delivery. I hadn't seen my primary doctor since the preterm labor incident. My next appointment was in two weeks, and I would see him then. By the time, two weeks had gone by. My hands were swollen, my feet were worse, my whole body was swollen; and I could hardly recognize myself when I looked in the mirror. When I got into the doctor's office that day, they did all the usual; but they had me pee in a cup, which was new. The doctor came into the room and told me I needed to go to the hospital immediately. I didn't understand the severity of the situation, so I refused. He sent me home on strict bed rest and told me to go straight to the hospital if I felt light headed. That evening, I almost passed out; so off to the hospital my mom and I went. I had no clue about the events that were about to take place or that I would be fighting for mine and my baby's lives in the days to come.

Here we are at the hospital. My mom pulls up and goes in to get a wheelchair. Here comes a man to get me, and we aren't stopping in the emergency room. "We are going up to the labor and deliver floor," he told me. Labor and delivery? Why are we going there? That's not where I went last time. It's too early to have my baby. I have six more weeks to go. They get me all settled in a bed. The nurse comes in and puts the blood pressure machine on me then the baby monitor on my belly, so I can her my baby's heartbeat. A sigh of relief when I hear it, I know everything is okay. The doctor walks in and tells me they have to give me medicine through an IV to start my labor. I have been diagnosed with full blown eclampsia, and the baby is poisoning me and has to be delivered now. Right now? It's too early. How will I know if my baby is going to make it? He tells me I won't know, and there is a strong chance the lungs won't be developed, but we won't know until the delivery. He goes on to tell me that my blood pressure is extremely high, so they have to give me another medicine through the IV that brings my blood pressure down. The problem is that the medicine for my blood pressure makes the medicine to start my labor not work as well; but we have no choice. This is what we have to do. I'm so scared, but I know I have to do what I have to do to save my baby. My mom calls our neighbor who is coaching me, and she comes right up to be with us.

They are here to start the IV and hook up the medicines. I'm trying to understand what is going on, but everything is going so fast. I'm just going to try to relax. I fall sleep for a little bit, but I'm woke up by the worst pain I've ever felt in my whole entire life, contractions. God help me. It hurts so bad. I'm told I can't have anything for pain yet that will slow my labor down as well as the blood pressure medicine. I have to tough it out for as long as I can. It was time to put to work the Lamaze breathing my coach had taught me, and she is right there to help me through. We start by timing the contractions so I will know how long it will be before the next one comes. Here it comes. She grabs my hand and looks into my eyes, and we breathe just like we practiced. In through my nose and push it out through my mouth, nice deep breaths to push through the pain, and it's gone. The night goes by, and now it's the next day. It's getting very hard for me to handle the pain. I beg the nurse to please give me something. A few hours later, the doctor comes in and orders me some pain medicine to be given through my IV. As soon as she gives it to me, I can't breathe. She pulls the oxygen mask out, puts it over my face, and lowers my bed down flat; and everyone came rushing in. I blacked out.

I wake up to pain again. Breathe, breathe, and breathe through the pain. What happened? What time is it? What day is it? The pain is unbearable. The nurse comes in and increases my medications again. "It's taking so long because the medications are fighting each other to work," she explains.

It's day two of labor, and I'm so exhausted; but my baby's heartbeat is strong, so I am okay. Now my head hurts. It hurts so bad I feel like it's going to explode. The nurse explains to me it's because my blood pressure is so high, and she gives me more pain medicine, but a different kind this time. The other medicine had made me stop breathing, so they wouldn't be giving me that again. I fall sleep and wake up to a feeling of being on fire. I'm so hot. They are putting cold wash clothes on my head and feet, and it's just not helping. I fall back to sleep. As I wake up, I see and hear my mom crying. The doctor had just been here, but I didn't remember why is she crying. My mom never cries. Something is wrong.

After the first night, my mom and my coach decided they would have to take turns in order for someone to always be with me. I have to tell you, my birthing coach was another one of my angels along the way. She did so much for me and asked nothing in return. My blood pressure was so dangerously high, and I was in such bad condition they didn't want me left alone. My mom was there the morning the doctor came and told her he wasn't sure if her daughter or grandchild would live through this. The baby was poisoning me, and it was looking bleak. My blood pressure was so high I was having small strokes also known as transient ischemic attacks. Labor was going so slow, and a C-section was not an option because I would not make it through the operation.

It's my third day in labor. I'm waiting for the doctor to come in. I am so tired and have been in this horrible pain for three days now. Here he comes, asking me how I am. Are you kidding me? I sit up and let him have it. "You want to know how I am? I need you to get this baby out of me today!" I cannot take it anymore, and I'm yelling at him. "Can't you just cut me open? I cannot handle it anymore. You have to do something, and I just begin sobbing. I have IV lines in both arms, and they are talking about starting one in my neck, blood pressure machine on my arm going off every ten minutes, baby monitor around my belly, catheter in because I can't get out of bed, no food or drink for three days now. I'm having excruciating back labor, and my head feels like it's going to explode because my blood pressure is deadly high. "Please, please help me," I plead. He tells me he can order an epidural, and I agree. After the epidural was in place, I was able to rest a little. Thank you, God. The contractions are strong now and very close together. The nurse comes in to check my dilation; and woo hoo, it's almost time to push. They take me into a surgical room to deliver. My doctor comes in and asked if medical students can come watch my delivery, and I agree. So here we are. I'm showing all I have and more to a bunch of strangers, and I do not care. I'm pushing with my contractions now, and everyone in the room is being so helpful. One hour goes by, two hours go by, and I am pushing with every contraction every couple of minutes. I am exhausted. The third hour comes, and I'm running out of push when one of the students offered me a mirror so I can see my baby's hair. Just a couple of more pushes, everyone is cheering me on. This was a miracle happening. We weren't supposed to make it to this point. One last push and out comes my beautiful baby girl! They take her and suction her. I'm asking, "Is she okay? Her lungs, is she breathing?" And a big huge cry came out of my baby girl, and another and another. I did it! She's the most beautiful baby I've ever seen, absolutely perfect. As she is lying on my chest for the very first time, I kissed her delicate little head and hold her so close. She smells beautiful. She feels so perfect in my arms. I've never felt a love like this before. I'm eighteen years old.

CHAPTER SIX

New Beginnings

After my delivery, I would spend the next three days in a private recovery room. I had gained over one hundred pounds in water, and my blood pressure was still deadly high, but we had made it. We lived! One of the nurses who cared for me in labor and delivery came to check on me. She said, "I never do this. Come check on my patients after delivery, but I was so worried about you. I had to come check on you," and she gave me a big hug. I can guarantee I have been a topic of her conversation throughout her life.

Yes, my baby was absolutely perfect in every way! I decided to breast feed her. That's the best thing for my new bundle of joy. The lactaid specialist came in and taught me everything I needed to know. We were doing great at first; but now, it isn't really working. My baby isn't eating, and she's losing weight. The doctor informs me they have to put a tube in her nose down to her tummy, and I will have to pump my milk and feed my baby through a syringe and tube. Anything you say to keep my baby alive and healthy.

One week after delivery, I was discharged home; but my newborn baby would have to stay in the neonatal intensive care unit a bit longer until she could eat on her own. I would pump at home and take my milk up to feed her during the day and leave some for the nurses to feed her at night. We did this for a week and a half and then we tried the bottle, and she was sucking! It was finally time for her to come home with me. The plan was discharge home the next day.

When I arrive at the hospital in the morning, I'm informed my baby is in an incubator under black lights and has Jaundice. She won't be coming home for a couple of more days now. I'm heartbroken, but it's only a couple of more days.

I settle myself into the wooden rocking chair. It's the same one I've been rocking my sweet baby girl in for the past week and a half. Her little head fits in the palm of my hand, and her body extends the length of my forearm. She is so tiny, so precious, so perfect. I can't wait to take her home. I can't keep her out for long because she needs to be under the lights. I enjoy the time I have today; and hopefully, she can come home with me tomorrow. This is it baby girl. It's me and you against the world. I won't ever have to feel lonely again because now I have you.

It was finally time to take my baby home. What a great day. We get home and get all settled in. Visitors come and go for the next few weeks, and I'll be graduating high school at the end of the month. Even though I was the talk of the school, being the only one to have had a baby, I didn't care what everyone thought about me. I took my butt to my graduation with my newborn baby, and I walked across that stage and got my diploma with my head held high, despite all the whispering going on about me. I have always been independent. I have always been a fighter. I have always figured out a way to get what I want. I wouldn't have survived without these qualities. I was raised in the Missouri Synod Lutheran Church, so baptism is customary for newborns.

We are to have our baptism ceremony at the end of the service this Sunday. I'm nervous but excited at the same time. I'm wearing the dress I wore for my graduation. It's white to match my baby girl's beautiful baptismal gown. My mom's best friend and her husband are the god parents. I grew up calling her best friend my aunt. I loved her like an aunt. She taught me so many things: how to make grape leaves, bulgoki, and escargot. How to play UNO and drink wine. I got my love for Mrs. Fischer's potato chips from her as well. She was a four-foot-eleven Greek lady with a huge afro and a British accent as she was raised in England. She was firry and feisty, and I loved her so much. I was honored to have her be my baby's godmom.

It's the day of the service. We arrive at the church early so we can talk with the pastor. It's the same church I've gone to all my life. The pastor greets us, and he goes over a practice service with us. We are then seated in the first two pews on the left hand side. It gets to our special part of the service, and he announces our baptism to the congregation and has us come up to the front of the church. I'm so nervous. Here we go. It's a packed service even the balcony is full. All these people here to celebrate my baby girl becoming part of Jesus's family. The smile on my face cannot be removed. I'm so proud, so happy. Pastor takes my baby and baptizes her in the name of the Father, Son, and Holy Spirit. She didn't cry at all. She loved the water. He placed her back in my arms and turned us toward the congregation to present us. I hear him saying words and more words. I'm only half paying attention because I'm so nervous with all these people looking at me, but I'm so proud at the same time. All of a sudden, I hear my pastor say, "May God forgive this child for having a baby out of wedlock." I can't believe what I just heard. I'm embarrassed and devastated. What kind of person does that to someone? Does he know what I've gone through to get here? Does he know I almost lost my life and my baby's life just a couple of months ago? Does he know that I graduated despite all the odds against me? Does he know I've fought tooth and nail to be here on this earth for the past sixteen years, obviously not. I never returned to that church. He disgraced me in front of the entire congregation, and there was no way to take that back.

Shortly after the baptism, the father of my baby girl got in contact with me, or I found him. I'm not really sure. He hadn't seen her yet, and she was already three months old. I took her to see him for the first time. He was living with a foster family, and they were helping him get his own apartment. A few weeks later, I was at home in the kitchen, and I'm not sure exactly how it went; but my father found out I was talking to my ex again and told me if I was going to talk to him. I wasn't allowed in his house. I packed up my baby and everything I could fit into my car and moved in with my baby's father in his new one bedroom apartment. So here I am, apartment, boyfriend, baby, job, and college student. I had so much going on, but I was with the father of my baby and was helping me take care of her now. I came home from work one night to hear my baby crying and crying. I picked her up and comforted her and calmed her down. Her father was frustrated and left when I got there. When I went to change her diaper, I found a bruise on her bottom. I couldn't believe my eyes. He had hurt my baby. When I confronted him about it. He told me he didn't realize how hard he was wiping her. I never left her alone with him again. I didn't leave because I had nowhere to go, but he never had her by himself again.

Something was wrong with me and my baby. She kept getting a cough, and I was constantly throwing up and couldn't keep anything down. I had taken her to her doctor and to the emergency room twice. One afternoon, she was coughing so much her lips were blue; and I called 911. The emergency room doctor diagnosed her with bronchitis and sent us home. I took her back to her pediatrician the next day and refused to leave until they figured out what was wrong with my baby. They finally figured it out. She had pertussis or whooping chough. She was immediately admitted to the hospital. The next day, I started throwing up blood and was admitted to the hospital for bleeding ulcers. They would not let us be in the same hospital because of our doctors, so I was in one hospital; and my baby was across town at another one. While in the hospital, I found out my boyfriend and father of my child was cheating on me and gave me a venereal disease. I had had enough. I was at my whit's end, and somebody was going to get it. I just so happened to be admitted to the hospital that told me my baby had bronchitis and sent me home with a critically ill baby. I found out that doctor's name and called down to the ER when he was on shift and gave him an ear full. I told him he misdiagnosed my baby when she had whooping cough, and it could have cost her life. I told him I was calling him so that in the future, he could avoid the same mistake. He both thanked me and apologized.

After I was discharged, I spent my days at the hospital with my daughter until she was discharged. I had my baby home, and she was recovering well. My stomach was healing well, but I was having problems with vaginal bleeding. Once I got my period after delivery, it never went away. I had been bleeding for months, so back to the doctor I went. They put me on birth control to try to regulate my period and then one other medication to stop the bleeding, but nothing worked. I was then scheduled for a dilation and curettage also known as a D&C. It's a surgical procedure where they clean out the lining of the uterus. This was the first surgical procedure I had since the chin cancer incident when I was three. I was so nervous, but I made it through. Stronger than ever.

I got my own apartment and left that dirt bag. He followed me. He conned me. He schmoozed me but not for long. One day, I was trying to get him out of my apartment. I just wanted him gone, and he just kept showing up like a lost puppy. Our argument escalated, and he pinned me down on the bed. I was trying to get him off me, but I wasn't strong enough. He said, "Remember when we told each other that no matter how mad we got at each other, we would just have sex about it and get over it?"

I said, "Yes, but I don't feel that way anymore. I have no interest in you or having sex with you. I just want you to leave me alone."

He said he didn't believe me and pulled up my skirt. I'm trying to get my legs up so I can kick him off of me. He unzips his pants and forces my legs open, and I start screaming. He covers my mouth with his sweaty hand and forces himself inside of me. Poof, I'm gone; and I don't have any memory for a few days. I never told anyone. I never went to the emergency room. I kept it to myself after all. I was used to men forcing themselves on me.

One night, I was hanging out with friends and met a new guy. We started hanging out a lot. He was sweet, considerate, funny; and he was great with my baby girl. I fell for him fast and hard, but it would only last a couple of months, and he moved to another state. It was around the same time. I got that dreadful phone call from my mom about my father molesting my sister. Something snapped in my mind. Up until this point, I had blocked all my childhood memories; and now, some of them came flooding back like a tidal wave. I hadn't tried to commit suicide for an entire year, but that would quickly change. I don't remember the specifics of this attempt, only what I've found in my medical records. Let me share my findings.

I was found unconscious by friends in my apartment, and they called 911. Upon arriving to the emergency room, I was lethargic and agitated, arousable but not communicative. I was intubated and placed in four-point leather restraints because I had become combative. "Her speech and thought process seemed within normal limits, but she seemed to be very defensive and immature," the doctor wrote. He went on to write, "She was extremely uncooperative, very angry, and irritated, overreactive at this time. And in my assessment, very unpredictable, realizing that she has taken an overdose in serious suicide attempt. Did not even inform anyone. I would suggest that she be transferred to the state mental facility after she is medically stable so that they could treat her for depression and rule out personality disorder."

I was admitted to the intensive care unit because I had put my heart in a tachycardia state, and chest x-ray showed enlarging of my heart and fluid in my lungs. Not to mention, I had gone bat shit crazy, four-point leather restraints? Are you kidding me? I would never act that way. I was quiet, shy, and polite. I am nineteen years old.

I would like to introduce you to Suzzie, my savior. I've told you about her. How she came into existence and the purpose she served in my life. Her personality is that of a fighter and protector, and she is a little girl. She is the little girl who took the worst abuse dealt out by my father and tried to fight him off for years and years. She is the one who saved me time and again and continues to step up and save me. She is a force to be reckoned with and is as fierce as a wild fire being fueled by the wind. She cannot be contained.

After I was stable enough to be discharged from the hospital, I was taken to the state mental hospital by the sheriff's department. I do not remember much about being there except for the crazy plastic furniture they had there. It looked like 1970s blow-up furniture. I used to play with my Barbies, but it felt like the consistency of clay. Each piece was a different color. There was an orange sofa, blue and green chairs, pink love seat. I liked it. I stayed inpatient here for two weeks. I still did not tell my secret. I missed my daughter so bad. My mom and sister were taking care of her while I was away. Once I was discharged from the state mental hospital, I vowed to start over, to give myself and my baby a new beginning. That is exactly what I did. I went back to school, got a new apartment, and a part time job. My mom had left my dad. She and my sister were living in a townhouse ten minutes away from me, so I spent a lot of time over there.

It was around this time that my sister came to visit, not the sister that came when I was a baby but the second to the youngest of their set of siblings. She had heard about my parents separating and came to check on us. This wasn't her first visit. I was about ten or eleven when she came and lived with us for about three weeks. I loved having a big sister and didn't want her to leave. She was told by our father that she could stay and live with us. He would get her a car and pay for her college with one stipulation. She had to cutoff contact with all her family back in Michigan. He wanted her to stop talking to her mom, brothers and sisters, aunts and uncles, cousins so that she could live with a father who walked out on her when she was just a little girl with a new family he had made. I don't blame her for leaving. I wish she could have stayed. I know she would have protected us, but he made her make a decision that was completely unfair, and he knew that. That's just the type of person he was, evil to the core. It would be many years before she came to visit me again and understandably so.

I met a new guy through some mutual friends, and he was amazing to my daughter and me. We had so much fun together. He's the only one I ever dated that my mom liked, and she still asks about him to this day. One night, we were hanging out; and we went on a scavenger hunt that a local radio station put on. We had to drive around the city listening to the radio station for the next clue. There were five of us in a car, a couple people I didn't know that well. The next thing I know, we are getting pulled over; and I am being hand-cuffed and arrested. One of the people in the car was a minor, not just any minor a runaway, not just any runaway minor, her father was my arresting officer. Now I didn't even know this girl, not even her first name. She was in the car when I jumped in, and she was with the driver, and he had just met her. That didn't stop that cop from cuffing me so tight that I had handcuff bruising around my wrist and then he told me he was going to take me out to a field and do what he wanted with me and dispose of my body, true story. But you see, I had endured so many similar threats from my father growing up that this guy didn't even phase me. I told him to go ahead, give it his best shot. He did nothing of the sort. I was arrested for contributing to the delinquency of a minor and bailed out within a couple of hours.

This was also around the time I went and got my first tattoo. It hurt so bad, but it hurt so good. I loved the pain, and I had a beautiful work of art on my body as a bonus. It was also around the time my cousin Lee started college at an art institute in Chicago. This is my cousin that was like my sister. We are only a couple of years apart in age and, we grew up together. We have very similar features, and everyone has always asked us if we are sisters. She is my mom's youngest brother's daughter. I would get on the train in a city close by one weekend night a few times a month and go visit her. Sometimes a couple of friends would come with, and we would drive into the city. We partied and had great times. It wasn't long before I was single again, and I stayed that way for a while. I concentrated on making a better life for my baby and myself.

It didn't take long before I ended up back in the hospital again from attempting suicide. This time, it would be a month stay and five days after discharge. I was right back again being admitted. I would be doing so well in life. At least I thought I was and out of left field. I was trying to kill myself. I was diagnosed as bipolar with borderline personality disorder. After all these hospital stays, I was seeing counselors and psychiatrists, participating in outpatient therapy groups; but I still wasn't telling anyone my secret. My sister had broken her silence, and I helped her escape the monster. I had been institutionalized time and again and never told. There was one time, I had overdosed on valium. I don't remember how I got it or actually taking the pills. I lost a whole week of time. I was caring for my daughter, making trips to Madison Wisconsin; and from what I'm told, I was seen going to the mall. One afternoon, I was at a friend's house, and a mutual friend stopped by. She proceeded to tell me about how she saw me at the mall and came up to me, and I didn't recognize her. She said she was calling out my name; and when she caught up with me, I looked at her crazy and told her I didn't know her. She also informed me I was acting funny, out of my normal character, childlike. I have absolutely no memory of it and wrote it off as everyone has a twin. She swore it was me. Now that I look back, I believe it was Suzzie.

Now it had been sometime since I had dated; but one day, I ran to the pizza joint on the corner to pick up dinner for my mom, my sister, my baby, and myself. That's when it happened. I met a guy. He was flirting with me the whole time. I was waiting in line; and when I got up to place my order, he asked for my phone number. Now he was older than me by eleven years, but everyone my age seemed to be useless. He was handsome, and he was interested, so why not? I gave him my number. We talked on the phone for a few weeks and started dating. It wouldn't be long before I found out he was living with another woman who he claimed was just a roommate. That was not the case at all, but it didn't stop me from trying to win him over and make him mine. That's exactly what I did.

I was twenty-two, and he was thirty-three. He said he had been previously married and had son that he didn't get to see often because they lived in a different state. He was the oldest sibling and spent a lot of time helping care for his younger siblings growing up. His mom and dad were divorced. His mom was a pastor. Those were the things about himself he disclosed to me, but there was so much more I didn't know about and had to learn the hard way. I would come to find out that he was illiterate. No, he could not read nor write. He told me it was because he stayed home from school to care for his siblings and never learned, so I tried to help. I got him a tutor at our local literacy council. He went twice and quit. He also failed to mention he was an alcoholic, and it wouldn't be long before I discovered he was a crack addict as well.

I must be completely honest. This was never a good relationship. It was always tumultuous even from the very beginning. He moved in with me a few months after us meeting, and I became pregnant quickly. I was excited and scared when I found out. I could only hope that what happened with my first pregnancy didn't happen with this one. I was excited to tell my man I was having his baby! Woo hoo, bun in the oven over here! His response was not what I expected. He told me I should have an abortion. Are you kidding me? Are you crazy? I absolutely will not do that. I am having this baby. I love my baby already, and I won't let you ruin that, and so it began.

I knew something funny was going on because my boyfriend was getting a ride home from his manager at work every night, and they were always making excuses about why he was late coming home. I confronted him one morning about it, and he beat me severely with a belt. I had belt mark welts and bruises all over my body; and when it was all over, when he had worn himself out from the blows he was delivering, he left; and I called the police. I was so embarrassed, degraded, and humiliated. They had to take pictures of me naked for evidence, and I was pregnant. I had turned my back to the strikes to protect my baby, you could see the welts and bruises in the form of belt marks starting on my upper back and going down to my ankles. I broke up with him only to take him back a few months later. He was sorry, and I was having his baby. He wouldn't do it again. He loved me. That's what he promised me and so I believed him.

One night, after he went to sleep, I went through his wallet only to find two tickets issued by the police for indecent exposure and breaking park curfew. One was issued to him, the other to his manager at work. I didn't say a word to him about it, but what I did do was have that woman's address now; and she was married. I found her house the next day. I pulled in the driveway and walked up to the door and knocked. When her husband answered, I just walked away. I didn't have the nerve to tell him what I had come to say. That wasn't the end of it though. It took me a couple of days, and I got up the nerve, and I went back over there.

Now I feel I must first disclose to you that while I could see what was going on, I felt like Suzzie was up front and in action. I was also seven months pregnant. When I arrive at her house, I see they are having a yard sale. I pull up in the driveway. All her family is there, her sister, her kids, the whole shebang. I get out of the car and approach his manager. She knows who I am because I would go up to his work all the time, and she would play nice to my face. I instantly start letting her have it. "You fucking bitch. You are fucking my boyfriend, and I'm about to have his baby."

She is pleading with me, "Please don't do this in front of my family and all these people. Isn't it enough you got me fired from my job?"

I respond by telling her she should have thought about that while she was fucking my boyfriend after work every night before going home to her family. I went on to say I hoped she enjoyed sucking and fucking my boyfriend's black dick because it was going to cost her family. And then her husband came out of the house and asked what was going on, to which I replied, "Your wife is having an affair with my boyfriend. He works with her. Didn't she tell you? That's why she lost her job. You see I'm pregnant, and she knew that too. You guys have a nice life."

With that, I got in my car and drove off. Yes, I had gotten her fired from her manager position by calling the corporate office and telling them exactly what was going at her store, and how she was using her position to have an affair on her husband with my boyfriend. I did not know she had lost her job until the moment she said it, but I kind of figured. As far as I was concerned, she got what she deserved.

I had kicked him out of the house and was trying to just live my life when I received a phone call one day. It was from my one of my best friends from high school. She would be the one who my first daughter's father cheated on me with; and subsequently, they ended up together. She was calling to tell me that he had died. He was in a fatal car accident in Florida. It didn't really affect me. It was kind of a relief. I could tell my daughter her father was dead instead of a deadbeat dad. There was also that fact that he raped me, so it was a relief to hear the news. It sounded too good to be true really, and I knew both of them very well, so I had a hard time believing the story.

When I checked into it, I found out it was a lie and confronted her. She spilled her guts and put him on the phone. He said they did it so I would stop trying to get child support from him. Guess what I did at this point. I let this man see his daughter. I thought maybe he was sorry. Maybe he had grown up. I let her go visit a couple of times; and the third time he came to pick her up, he wouldn't tell me where he was taking her. He didn't have a phone number where I could reach him this time, so I refused to let him take her. As I was walking away from his car with my four-year-old in my arms; and I am seven months pregnant, he tried to run me down with his car. If I had not jumped out of the way, he would have hit all three of us. Never again, he would never be allowed back in our lives.

We had only been separated for about six weeks; but when my boyfriend wouldn't leave me alone and kept begging to come back, I finally caved in. He wasn't going hit me or call me names or cheat anymore. He wanted to do right by his children. I took him back. I was scared and nervous, but I was about to have his baby, and all I wanted was a loving family even if I didn't know what one looked like.

Well folks, it wouldn't be too much longer until he was up to his old tricks again; and when I say not too much longer, I mean less than a month. I don't even remember all the specifics of how I found out about him cheating again or how I found out where the girl lived, but I did. Yes, I paid her a visit; and yes, I was eight months pregnant when I did the following. She lived in a second-story apartment of an old Victorian house. I pull up and get out of the car. I climb up two flights of stairs and knock on the door. As she cracks the door to answer it, I step back and kick it in, pushing her back. I gain entry to the apartment and begin to attack her. I chase her all around the apartment and back down the stairs and around her yard until I can't run anymore. She swore she didn't know about me and said she would leave him alone. None of that mattered because when I got home, I pulled a waiting to exhale on his ass and set all his shit on fire in the backyard and changed the locks. I called him up and told him not to bother coming back. There was absolutely nothing left for him here, and I hung up the phone. I am now going to be a single mom of two children. I am twenty-two years old.

TWO SHORT-SLEEVED ONES AND A SWEATSHIRT

March 3-94
Tried to kill myself, unsuccessful
obriously. I'm okay now. My man
is watching Tracy for me. I'm
going to Tracy's by myself. Bummer
but i'm miss her. I took twenty valium a
9:30 this morning & i woke up at
6:00 at night. I f... gotten tard, but
my out burst makes me feel better.

March - 14th 317 Lm.

Sadly i don't remember writing the previous

CHAPTER SEVEN

Happily Never After

Can you believe it? I made it to twenty-two, woo hoo! It's a couple of days after my birthday, and I'm headed to the doctor. Only a month left and my new baby will be in my arms. I don't find out the gender because I love surprises, and there is no better surprise than to see what I'm having at the time of birth. The nurse calls me back and has me do the routine pee in a cup, takes my blood pressure, and informs me the doctor will be in shortly. He comes in a sits down on his stool and informs me I have to be at the hospital tomorrow morning at five thirty to induce my labor. I have high amounts of protein in my urine, which is a sign of preeclampsia, and my blood pressure is high. Here we go again. I'm nervous and scared. It's a month early, but I have no choice. I can only hope this goes more smoothly than last time. Because my baby's father is not in the picture, I ask the coach I had for my first baby to assist me again as well as one of my good friends. I go home and call them both and call my mom so she can free her schedule to watch my daughter. Now to get ready for the morning, bag packed, check; my own comfy pillow, check; strength, check; and big-girl panties, check. I'm all ready.

I arrive at the hospital as instructed. My friend came with me, and my coach was to show up later. They get me all hooked up with the IV, baby monitor around my belly, there is the heartbeat no better music to a mommy to bees' ears. It's not too long before I start having contractions. I have chosen to do it natural. Everything is going smooth, and then the nurse comes in to check me. She's having a hard time finding the heartbeat, so she gets and internal fetal monitor that goes on the baby's head. Ah, there it is. Everything's okay.

A couple of hours go by, and I'm hanging in there, I'm getting up and sitting in the rocking chair, and the nurse asked if I want to take a bath in the whirlpool tub. Of course, I do. That sounds like a great idea. She's running the water when, all of a sudden, she has me get back in bed. My baby's heartbeat has dropped drastically. I'm instructed to get on my hands and knees in the bed. That's not helping. Now I flip over. That's not helping either. The nurse runs out and returns in less than a minute. Next thing I know, they are pushing my bed down the hallway and an anesthesiologist is asking me a bunch of questions. "What's wrong? What's going on?" I asked. I'm told I'm being taken for an emergency C-section. My baby's heartbeat is fading. They move me over to the operating table, put a mask on face. And I'm gone.

When I wake up, the first thing out of my mouth is "Is my baby okay?"

The recovery room nurse tells me, "Yes, everything is fine."

The next question, "Is it a girl or a boy? A girl, it's a girl, and she's okay? Thank God. Thank God. Thank God, my baby is okay. What happened? Why did her heartbeat go down? What was wrong?"

She tells me that the umbilical cord had gotten wrapped around her chest and neck, and it was strangling her, but they got her out on time. It was at that moment that the pain hit. I felt like I had been cut open with a blade of fire. "Hey, when can I see my baby? I need my baby. I need to be holding her. Please get her for me." I had to wait a few more minutes; but when they placed her in my arms, I melted. My beautiful baby girl, so perfect in every way. I can't kiss her enough. I check her over all her tiny fingers, all her tiny toes, and then I turn her over and see bruises on her back. I instantly freaked out. "What happened to my baby? Why is she bruised?"

The nurse explains they are not bruises, they are birthmarks called mongoloid spots. They are common in babies of mixed race. Thank goodness, because it was about to go down in that recovery room.

Although there were complications, and I had to have an emergency C-section, I was happy because everything turned out okay. My mom brought my daughter up to the hospital to meet her new sister. She sat beside me in the bed and held her little sister in her arms for the first time. What a beautiful picture. She even got to feed her all by herself. She's going to be a great big sister. I tried preparing her by carrying around a baby doll and talking lots about the new baby coming. I even set the old crib up so that she could sleep in it while her sister was in the bassinet. I didn't want her to feel like the baby got all the attention. They stay for a while, and its bedtime soon; so they go home.

My sister and her friend had come up, so they stay and visit for a while longer. While they are visiting, in walks my new born baby's father. Wait, that's not it, he's not alone. Remember that girl I chased all over? She was with him and holding a stuffed teddy bear. Are you fucking kidding me? This bastard has some nerve, but you want to know what? I wasn't going to act a fool in the hospital with a newborn, post C-section. So I ate it. I gobbled down all the hate, anger, and rage I was feeling for my baby. I'm sure it helped that the drugs going in my IV were pretty good too. I let him hold her. It was after all his baby. They didn't stay long; and as soon as they left, I threw that fucking stuffed bear in the trash. What a piece of shit. Who does that?

Well, I will tell you who does some disrespectful garbage like that. The man I will marry and just a few short months. Yes, you read it right. I marry him. I would love to tell you how it came to be, why I took him back; and that there was a romantic proposal, but I cannot do that. I don't remember. I know that here I was with two children by two different fathers, and I just wanted a family to call my own. I wanted to give my children the love I never received, and I wanted to be loved. The problem was, I had no idea of what real love looked like, only what I had been taught.

I was discharged from the hospital a couple of days after the birth of my beautiful baby girl. By this time, my mom had taken my sister and moved back in with my father. I was told he apologized to her, and it would never happen again. My mom promised and swore that she would keep her eyes and ears open, and she would never let it happen again. She also swore to protect my children from him. When my oldest daughter went over there, she was never left in a room alone with him; and if she stayed the night, my mom slept with her. I know you have to be wondering how I allowed that, and I do to. I will let you know now that my children grew up idolizing that man and that my mom did what she said and protected my children. I have asked them, and they deny he ever did anything to them. To them he was a hero.

It wasn't too long after I came home that my brother moved to town. He was the third born out of five from my father's first wife. We immediately clicked, and he moved in with me. He got a job at the hospital I was working at. It felt great to have a big brother. He was great with my kids. We lived together, worked together, and had so much fun. It would only make sense for him to stand up for me at my wedding, and he did. My father wasn't going to come. He didn't come to the hospital for the birth of either of my daughters, and he wouldn't show up for my wedding. It was perfectly fine by me because I hated his fucking guts anyway. I'll tell you when he did show up, each and every time I was in a psychiatric hospital. I think he came for two reasons, to make his presence known to me and to give me the illusion that he gave crap. Both were manipulations to keep me quiet, and it worked.

Now where were we? Ah, yes, I'm getting married! I will finally have the love and family I've always yearned for. What could be better than this? I know, I know, this guy hasn't always been the best; but I'm sure that will change once we say I do. It's the big day. I'm not about being fancy. I'm a rather simple soul, so we are getting married in our backyard, and I'm barefoot. Everyone is here, my mom, sister, cousin, brother, and my babies. The charge nurse at the hospital I'm employed at is also a pastor. She and her husband are here to perform the ceremony for us. The ceremony is short and sweet. We exchange vows and rings and, bam! Just like that. I'm hitched. Yes, I really did marry a man who was eleven years my senior, who abused me physically, mentally, and emotionally. A man who lied and cheated, who is an alcoholic and drug addict. Yes, I really did. I found a man who would treat me just like my father did, and I married him. I am twenty-two years old.

Come with me. I'll be your tour guide in this story of my happily never after. It's our wedding night. My mom is watching the kids so my new husband and I can have some alone time on our wedding day. We aren't having a honeymoon, so it's the least she could do she says. I put on something sexy and snuggle up with my new husband in bed. After a few moments of me rubbing and touching on him, trying to get him in the mood, he turns his back to me and falls asleep. I instantly think to myself, *Oh, no, what have I done? I've just made the biggest mistake of my life. This man doesn't really love me.* All I've ever wanted is to be loved. I cry myself to sleep on my wedding night. I wake up with a heaviness on my chest, realizing the huge mistake I've made. Instead of running away like a woman, trying to escape a house of horrors, I sit at the edge of the bed. I take a deep breath in, and I tell myself, "Put your big-girl panties on. You made your decisions. Now make the best of it." Just like I learned from my mom.

It wasn't long before he was up to his old tricks, always leaving and staying gone for days. He would come home and start arguments with me. He didn't keep a job for longer than a couple of weeks. I was working and raising the kids and keeping up the house. I was so overwhelmed; so one night, my mom took the kids for me so I could have a break. I knew he had taken off for the weekend and with my babies in my mom's care. I decided to kill myself. I'm not sure what makes me decide to take my own life. It's like a switch flipping in my head. I was a failure, a failure in every way possible. My children would be better off without me. I take the keys off the kitchen counter and walk out to the garage. I open the car door, get in the driver seat, and shut the door. With the key in the ignition, I turn it over and roll down all the windows. I recline the seat and close my eyes. The smell is so strong but then I drift off to sleep. The next thing I know, I'm falling out of the car; and I begin crawling to the garage door. I can't get up. God, I'm so sick. I feel like I'm dreaming. My body is heavy. It's hard to move my arms and legs. I manage to pull myself up to open the door; and somehow, I get in the house and into bed. I drift back off to sleep. As I start to wake up, I realize I'm alive. The taste in my mouth is of pure exhaust. That's all I smell when I breathe in. I fight to keep my eyes open. I have to call my mom and tell her I'm sick and ask her to keep the kids one more night. If she finds me like this, she will know I tried to kill myself. How did I get out of that car? I feel like someone pulled me out and willed me to live. I should have died. I never told anyone about that serious attempt on my life. I've kept it a secret all of my life, until this moment as I am sharing with you.

It has been five months since I had my first period after the birth of my baby, and I'm still bleeding. Not this again. Yes, this again. I go to the doctor where I am informed I will have to have another D&C. While I'm waiting for my surgery date to come, my husband takes my car and is out driving without a license. Not only was he pulled over and arrested for driving without a license, but the state's attorney picked up my case and filed charges for domestic abuse. He had a warrant for when he beat me with a belt, and I still found a way to bond him out of jail. A couple of days later, I have my surgery. It's an outpatient procedure, so I am able to return home after with just a couple of days off work. It's back to life as normal, getting the kids up for school and day care, making breakfast, dropping kids off, going to work, and wondering what my husband is up to all day. I get off work, pick the kids up, head home where I will help with homework, and prepare dinner. They have playtime and bath time; and before you know it, it's bedtime. That was our daily routine.

Because we lived in a two-bedroom apartment, it was getting cramped as my brother still lived with us; so we decided to move into a house. My best friend and I decided to move in together, and my husband agreed. We found a house, and all got moved in. My friend and I had daughters the same age. She and I worked together, and our girls went to school together. We got tattoos together. This was my first legitimate tattoo from a shop. A tribal band on my right ankle. We hung out a lot together and had a great time. My husband was never home, so she kept me company, and we helped each other with the kids. It wasn't too long after we moved that my brother just went missing in action one day. I didn't know where he went; and he never came back, just like that. This was around the same time I found out I was pregnant again.

My period is late, but it's never normal. I decide to get a home pregnancy test just to check. Sure as shit. That sucker came back positive. I'm going to have another baby! Maybe it will be a boy this time. I'm so excited! I wait for my husband to come home so I can share the great news. When he arrives home, he goes up to the bedroom; and I followed. As he sits on the bed, I stand in front of him and told him, "I have some great news, I am pregnant!"

Once again, I'm given the response that I should have an abortion; and once again, I refuse. I already love this baby, I can't wait to hold my new baby; and no one, not even my husband, can steal that joy away from me. Now that my brother has gone and our family is expanding, we decide it best to get our own apartment; so my friend and I part ways on living together. In just a couple of months, we find a place, a nice two-bedroom lower apartment in a two family flat. I'm packing and preparing for the move when I discover I'm bleeding vaginally. I go to the hospital immediately where they verify my pregnancy and tell me I'll just have to wait and see if the baby hangs on or not. I have to be on bed rest. How am I going to move on bed rest? Luckily, my family helped me make the move. My husband never showed up to help move.

This was the time before cellphones; so when my husband didn't show up at home, I went out looking for him. It's my day off work, and the kids are in school and day care, and I am on a mission. I figure out where my husband has been hiding out at his cousin's house. I drive over to his apartment and knock on the door. I can hear movement, so I know someone is in there. I begin banging on the door; but no answer, so I kick it in. To my surprise, my husband nor his cousin were there; but there is a girl sitting on the couch looking terrified. I snatch her up by her shirt and make her spill her guts. She confirms she is dating my husband. I smack the shit out of her and begin trashing the entire apartment. When I'm done, I get her to tell me where he is and off I go. Upon locating my husband walking down the street, I pull into a parking lot, flag him down, and he walks up to my window. I precede to tell him where I had just come from and what I just did, and he replied by telling me I'm tripping and walks off. What did he just say? Oh hell, no, I'll show you tripping mother fucker. I put the car in reverse, back up a good distance, put it back in drive, and slam on the gas pedal. I'm headed full force ahead, and he doesn't even see it coming because he is walking with his back to me. Bam, up he flies with the impact of the car and down to the ground he goes. I yell out the window, "Now that's tripping, you piece of shit, and take off to pick my babies up!"

It wasn't long before we made up, and he agreed to go to treatment so that he could come home. This wasn't his first time in treatment or the first time I made him go as a stipulation to our marriage. He would always go for a few days and then leave. I learned to call up there and see if he was still there. When he would leave, he wouldn't come home. He would go out on the streets again and use. I call up to the treatment center and find out he has left. It was two days ago. I have to find him. Our baby is due soon. He eventually comes home, and it's time for me to go be induced to have our baby. I have to deliver early again because of signs of preeclampsia; but this time, my husband is with me like it's supposed to be. I'm so excited. We get up to the floor, and they get me all hooked up to all the usual machines. I've already talked with my doctor about having the baby all natural as I am going to have a tubal ligation done after the birth, and this will be my last baby. It's not recommended to have a natural birth after a C-section, and it's called V-back. I know this is my last baby, and I want the full experience of child birth, no C-section, no drugs. Here we go. I've been in labor all day; and as the evening approaches, the contractions are getting closer and stronger. The nurse comes in and checks me, and it's almost time to push. I wake my husband up as he has fallen asleep, surprise, surprise. The nurse suggests placing a catheter to drain my bladder and then the baby will come out. I ask her if she has called the doctor in to deliver first. She did not do as I asked and drained my bladder anyway. Almost immediately, I had to push; and there was no doctor in sight. She's making me hold the baby in through the pushes. I finally looked at her and said, "You get a doctor stat, or I'm delivering this baby on my own. Do you know what stat means?" I yell at her.

She grabbed a passing by doctor from the hallway. He came in. One or two more pushes, and I'm there. This doctor didn't have time to perform an episiotomy, and he used his finger to rip me. I sat straight up and swung at him. Fortunately, he was quick and dodged the punch. Last push and here comes my baby. It's a girl! My beautiful baby girl. She has a full head of hair, Oh my goodness. It's true about the heartburn. She's so perfect except that she is ghostly white. The nurse took her, and the doctor told her to give my baby a Narcan shot because she was held into long. I get her back everything is okay. She's healthy, so am I.

She's absolutely perfect! All her little fingers and toes are here. When I'm checking her over, I notice she has the same birthmarks as her sister. This time, I'm already educated so I know what they are. Most of all my husband was there with me the whole time. What a beautiful beginning. She is born on my grandmother's birthday, so she will have her name for a middle name. Because my husband and I can't agree on a name, this baby girl has two middle names. I am scheduled to have a tubal ligation tomorrow. This little bundle of joy will be my last. I'm so blessed to have three beautiful girls. Watch out world. Here we come!

A few months go by and it's almost Christmas, and I just want my family to have a nice Christmas. My husband has gone out and not come home once again. He finally comes home one day, and I just keep my cool because I want to have a nice Christmas. It's Christmas Eve; and against my advice, my husband takes the car up the street to the little market on the corner while I'm home with the kids. I answer the phone, and it is my husband telling me he was in a car accident up the street, and he was going to jail. I had to walk up the street and get the car. He was begging me to get bond money. We had Christmas without him, not because I didn't try to get him out, but because the banks weren't open to cash my paycheck. Once he was booked his bond went up and I couldn't get him out, I would have to save the money. I needed to keep my family together no matter how broken it was. While he was sitting in jail, I was home raising three kids on my own. I was having a hard time making ends meet, but I was used to it by now. My gas was shut off, leaving us in a home with no heat in the middle of winter. I asked my parents for help, and they denied me, so I got electric heaters and made due. My one-and a-half-year-old caught pneumonia. I have no heat. My husband is in jail, and I have a six-year-old and a baby to boot. Just when I think it can't get any worse. I won't stop bleeding after my last daughter's birth and have to have another D&C. I'm not sure how, but we got through it.

Finally, my husband is out of jail. I'm not sure why I expected him to step up to the plate now when he never had before, but I did. You see, I didn't get help with the kids when they were babies. I got up all night long for feedings and did them through the day as well. It was like I had four kids, and my husband was the hardest to care for. Once again, I was disappointed. Almost as soon as he got out, he was running wild again. One day, when I got home from work and picking up the older two girls, I expected my husband to be at home with our baby; but he wasn't. A few minutes later, he comes in the door with the baby in her car seat and sits her down. I unbuckle her and pick her up to hug her, and I smell something. It's a familiar smell. I've smelt it on my husband a hundred times, and I instantly become furious. I put the baby back in her car seat and escort the girls to their room, turn on a movie, and tell them to play and not come out until I open the door. I then go back to the living room where my husband is and asked him why it is that my baby smells like crack cocaine. Before he could even open his mouth to provide me with lie, I punch him straight in the jaw. This is for being the shitiest father in the entire world. I then picked him up and threw him into a wall and proceeded to choke the living shit out of him. This is for every time you called me a fat bitch, worthless piece of shit, and horrible mother. I finished it off with a few more punches to the gut, opened the front door, and threw him out. I told him to never come back, not this time, not ever. Consider your family gone forever. I opened the door to my three beautiful baby's room, removed the baby from the car seat, and examined her, hugged my baby girls, and went to the kitchen to cook dinner. I had cried so many tears in the past. I had none left to shed. I am now a single mother of three beautiful girls. I am twenty-four years old.

I did not take the baby to the hospital. I didn't want to get my children taken away; instead, I stayed up and watched my baby through the night for the next few nights. A couple of months go by and he harasses me over the phone but stays away. I filed for divorce but was awaiting the court date. I went back to school so that I could afford to raise my babies on my own. I was working full-time during the day and going to college in the evening. The weekends and nights were spent with my babies. Life was good. I was losing weight and really loving life without him around.

One morning, I was just getting up and making coffee. It was before I got the kids up. There was a knock at the door. I was always cautious because I was terrified that he would come back and try to kill me. I look out the curtain on the door and no one is there. I head back to the kitchen when the knock comes again. I return to the front door, look out again, and again no one is there. I think maybe it's the neighbor girl, and I'm not getting to the door fast enough, so I open the door to look around the corner and Bam! He grabbed me by the neck and forced me back in the house, threw me on the ground when he turned to shut the door, I scrambled across the floor to get to the phone in the living room. He beat me to it and yanked the cord out of the wall. I tried to run, but there was nowhere to go, and my babies were in the other room sleeping. He beat me and when I say beat me, I mean brutalized me. I took punches to the head, arms, back, chest, stomach, legs. He was relentless, I just tried to get away in the space I had, tried to protect myself the best I could. He beat me pretty bad, and he had me under the dining room table. I was on my back, and he had me pinned down. He was punching me in the private area, and I tried to be quiet for my kids, but I couldn't help it. I yelled out; and when I did, he placed his hands around my neck and began to squeeze, tighter and tighter. I can't breath. I can't move. I can't scream.

I was just about to lose consciousness when I hear my two-year-old say, "Daddy, Daddy, what are you doing to Mommy?" She had crawled out of her crib and opened her bedroom door. He let go of my neck, got up, and ran out the front door. My baby had saved my life. I grabbed her up and told her everything was okay. I kissed her little face and proceeded on with my day of getting the kids up and ready for day care. Once I dropped them off, I went home, fixed the phone cord, and called the police. Once the police came, I filed charges and went down to the court house and got and order of protection.

Here I am, twenty-four years old, three children—two of which are in diapers—and I'm halfway done with college. I receive no help from their fathers. There are many days that my meals consist of the scraps off my children's plates or nothing at all. As long as they are fed, that is all that matters. What am I going to do? I have to give my babies a good life somehow. One day, my mom makes me an offer to move back home while I finished my schooling. I have one year left. I agree to take their help on one condition that she keep her promise and that she knows I will call the police if anything happens to my kids. At this time, I decide to change my major. I had to be able to make enough money to support my kids on my own, so I decided to become a funeral director.

CHAPTER EIGHT

For the Love of Women

Mortuary school was four days a week, eight hours a day for one year, and one and a half hours drive from home. I had to have a part-time job because I still needed to provide for my children. I found a job at a local tanning salon working third shift. My routine went as such. I would get off work at five thirty in the morning, get kids up for day care, make breakfast, drop kids off, drive to school, after school drive home, pick up kids, go home, have dinner, give baths, help do homework. After a nap for a couple of hours, I got up and went to work. It was nice that it was only four days a week. That gave me time with my babies and a little time for a social life now that I was single. I vowed I wasn't going to let a man hurt me again, ever. I was single and ready to mingle as the saying goes.

One of my good friends from work, Tara was having a birthday party at her house; so I packed up the children and off we went. All of her family was there, and I hadn't met them before, so I was a little nervous. She had a daughter close in age to my oldest, so they played well together. One of her cousins had a son, my middles age; and she was a single mom as well. Once we started talking, the nervousness went away. We had a great time.

A couple of days later, I received a call from Tara asking if it was okay to give her cousin my number. She wanted to hang out and a have couple of drinks. Of course, she can have my number. I'm in the market for new friends, and I needed a girl's night out. She called, and we set up night to go out. This was a time before cellphones and navigation systems, so I called my new friend before I left to meet her. She gave me the directions to the bar, and I wrote them down on a piece of paper to take with me. While we were on the phone, she asked if it was okay for her friend to accompany us. He was her ex-boyfriend, but now they were friends. I thought it was a little strange; but who am I to judge? Of course, it was. I gave myself a look once over in the mirror; and I was one hot tammali, not to brag or anything. I had lost one hundred pounds after the birth of my last daughter and had survived with my life from an abusive marriage. For the first time in a long time, I felt good about myself.

I arrive at the bar and check myself out in the visor mirror before I go in. Let's pause for a moment because I need to share something with you and is as good as time as any. I do not like looking at myself in mirrors, and I do not like my picture taken. You see, when I look in the mirror, I don't like what I see; and many times, I don't feel like the person looking back at me, is me. This particular time, it felt good to look in the mirror. I give myself wink, a duck face pose, and get out of my car. I straighten out my clothes from the car ride and go into the bar. I greet my friend and her ex-boyfriend, and we order drinks. After a few drinks and some good conversation, the music starts up; and we begin dancing and having a great time. There is something about dance music that moves my soul. The bass makes me feel free. About an hour in, I excuse myself to the bathroom; and my friend accompanies me. As we are in the stalls, she asked me if I've been with a woman before. I tell her, "No, I haven't." I can't believe what I'm hearing. Is she really asking me this? She then asked if I've ever had a threesome before, to which I reply that I haven't. Oh my god, is this what this whole night is about? As we are at the sink washing our hands, she then asked me if I would consider it. I told her I would have to think about it. I would be so nervous, and she assures me she will make me feel comfortable. A few hours and a few drinks later, she invites me back to her place; and I decided, why not. I get in my car and am following them back to her apartment. I can't believe what is about to happen. I'm nervous but excited. They picked me. They actually saw me and thought she looks amazing and like a lot of fun. Guess what I turned out to be exactly that.

We had an amazing time that night. It unlocked something inside of me, a side I had never seen before, an uninhibited sexually charged succubus of sorts. I was on fire. There were many more nights like that one. We were having a good time. Linnea and I spent our own time together as well. It was with her that I got my third tattoo. A tribal sun with Japanese conji to mourn on my lower back. I was in mortuary school, and my grandmother had just passed; so it seemed practical. Now, because we were spending so much time together and having sex, I started to develop feelings for her. One day, I arrive at her apartment because she invited me over. When I walk in, she introduced me to her new friend who was a girl; and they were holding hands. I guess she set me straight real quick. I packed up my daughter and went home. We remained friends, but I kept my distance.

There were three of us girls who made it a point to go out every Saturday night. We were all single moms, so it was a release. Often times, we used the same sitter for all our kids and let our hair hang down. Now, when I say let our hang down, I mean we got loose. We got loose with guys and each other. We mixed it up. I had a lot of sex with many different people. I felt like a hippie in the sixties. Free love over here! There were many, many Saturday nights filled with drunken fun. Many of them are blurry, and some I just don't remember. There are people I had sex with that I cannot recall their names or their faces. If I would run into them on the street, I would continue on and know no different. I am in no way bragging. It is important that you see the damage that child sexual abuse does to its victims. I put my life in danger over and over again with no second thoughts about it.

Nevertheless, I would like to share a few of those nights with you. I'll start with the schoolteacher I met out one night. I don't usually go for short men, but there was something about this guy. I never dated him per say. He had a live-in girlfriend that I didn't find out about until later in the game. He was always popping up at every bar we were at. One night, we decided to have a make out session that turned into sex at the bar. We went looking around for a place and ended up in the time clock closet. It was after eleven, so who would punching in? Well guess what, we were right in the middle of it when the closet door opened; and there stood a stunned employee. His response was no worries I can wait, and he shut the door. I love the thrill of being able to get caught, and my fantasy was fulfilled that night. What a rush.

We usually met up at my friend Tara's house to predrink and get ready before heading out to our favorite night club. My favorite thing about this spot is that it had a barber's chair. It's a real barber's chair. You sit in the chair, the bartender lays it back, and pours the shot straight in your mouth, and then slams the chair up, making the alcohol fly down your throat. Yes, that was my jam right there. I loved going out dancing. I loved the music and feeling free.

This particular night, we were all out on the dance floor; and these guys keep trying to dance with us, but I am ignoring them. It is bar time, so we head out to the car; and these guys are calling us and chasing us, so we stop to talk. One guy is Scandinavian-looking, blond hair, piercing blue eyes and tan. The other has dark hair and blue eyes. Both are attractive, but the blonde looks like a Calvin Klein model, and they are about five years younger than us. They invite us back to their house to hang out, and we agree. We jump in Tara's red convertible. Even though it is cold outside, she puts the top down; and as we take off down the road, I get on the trunk and pretend I'm surfing. One of my friends pulls me down into the car and off we go. As we are walking into their house, we are informed to be quiet because their parents are home. Are you kidding me? I'm drunk, so I don't really care. We head down to the basement of a rather large home. We are all hanging out, and one thing leads to another. I end up riding the blonde guy like a bucking bronco on a toilet. Well, I must have been loud because, all of a sudden, we herd, "Boys, what are you doing to that poor young girl down there?" She is talking about me. Oh shit, I have to hide here. She comes down the stairs. I found a spot under some lawn chairs in the storage room. So here I am, naked and lying on a cold cement floor. Thank goodness she didn't see me. She goes back upstairs, and we finish what we were doing but just a little less loudly.

I must have given him my phone number because, one night, he called my house. He wanted to date me. I was completely flattered of course, but I had to be honest with him. I told him I was flattered, but I had three small children, was newly divorced, and in college. He was completely shocked. He would have never guessed I had three kids, but he understood and wanted to remain friends. We actually made friends with these guys and continued hanging out with them weekend after weekend. It got crazier and crazier and involved more guys. We were having sex in front of each other, basically having orgies almost every weekend. When I wasn't hanging out with this group of friends, I was hanging out with friends from college. I had sex with a couple of different guys in my class through the course of that year. I was spending time with my friend's cousin alone and with her ex-boyfriend. When I say spending time, I mean sexy time. Another particular night, we went over to one of my old friend's house where he was having a party. I do not know all the particulars of what happened, but I will tell you what I do remember of this night.

We were drinking and smoking weed; and somehow, I ended up naked in a bondage swing in front of; and entire room of people and everyone was taking turns whipping me with a horse whip and writing on me with permanent marker. I remember parts of it, but I was going in and out. At some point, my friend Tara said enough was enough and took me down and took me home. I felt as though I was watching the scene from outside my body. When I woke up at Tara's the next day, I had no idea where the marker writing had come from. She had to tell me what had happened. I felt ashamed and embarrassed. I did that, me? I couldn't believe it, but it was true. I'm so thankful she was there to take care of me. She is another one of my angels. There were many nights she looked out for me, and I'm sure she saved my life on more than one occasion.

On the flip side of this wild child was the mom who took her kids places and did fun stuff. I'm not sure how it all came about, but I decided to pack up my babies and hop a flight to Los Angles,

California to visit my cousin. I bought the girls matching dresses so that I could keep track of them at the airport. They are purple, my favorite color, with small flowers. Look at my girls. They are so beautiful, so cute. They are my life. I love them more than anything in the world. I'm unsure of how we traveled to the airport, but I remember being there. I remember how excited I was to be making this journey with my babies. We stayed with my cousin a couple of nights and then at a hotel a couple of nights. We went to Disneyland and to Hollywood. It was a very freeing experience. We had so much fun on that vacation. It felt great to be alive.

After I graduated from mortuary school and passed my state boards, I was on the search to find a job. I mailed out my resume to every funeral home in town and the surrounding towns. I called and followed up, but there was no one willing to hire and apprentice right now. I couldn't wait to get a job as a funeral director, so I went back to what I knew. I got a job at a local hospital as health unit coordinator on their cardiac unit. I found a house to rent and my babies, and I were out on our own again. I stopped going out to the bars on the weekend and spent my time at work, home, and taking the girls to activities. I enrolled them in swimming lessons, basketball, tumbling, anything they wanted to try. I got back in touch with one of my friends I hadn't seen in a while. To make a long story short, she moved in with us. Her daughter was the same age as my second, and they were inseparable. This is something I have done all my life, help people. It seemed I was always taking my friends in and helping them when they were down and out. I've always wanted to save the world even though I couldn't save myself.

Now, my friend Camilia and I weren't going out much; so one night, she invited a couple of friends over. They were our age—one male, one female. I don't recall if they were dating or just friends. We had a pool table in the basement, so we were down there shooting pool, listening to music, and having a few drinks. I'm not even sure how it happened; but the next thing I know, we are all in my bed having an orgy. I don't remember how the night ended or the next day began. What was crazy was that they showed up the next night, uninvited, knocking on the door. We didn't let them in.

It was just a couple of months after this that my friend found her own place and was able to move. Shortly after that, I was offered a position as an apprentice funeral director at a local funeral home. My big break had finally come. I was so excited. I went in for my interview and got the job. Now I had interviewed with one other funeral home in town who would not give me the job because I was a single mom of three children.

When I received this position, I was thrilled. I put my all into it. I absolutely loved being a funeral director. I loved the science of the embalming, and I loved helping people in their time of need. I had finally arrived. All the hard work I had put in to get to this point had finally paid off. I had only been there a couple of months when I was asked if I knew anyone who would be able to work part-time at the funeral home. The requirements would be to assist directors with removals, work visitations, and funeral services. You won't believe who I asked to come work with me, my father. Yes, I did; and I have a hard time wrapping my mind around it, but I got him a job, and I worked with him. You have to understand that I was raised all my life with this abusive, child-molesting man. He was my father. I wasn't rescued instead it was the opposite. I was hand fed to him. I believed this was just how life was. This man who had hurt me so bad in life was still my dad. It sickens me really.

Everyone that worked there loved my dad, thought he was the most upstanding citizen around; and most of the other funeral home staff employed there were men. There was one man in particular that kept making advances at me. He would say sexually inappropriate things to me, and I let him know that it was not okay at all. He didn't take me serious, and it escalated to him touching me inappropriately. After a few times of him grabbing my ass and me telling him it wasn't okay and to stop, I had finally had enough. I went to the manager and filed a complaint. It wasn't long before he resigned.

I was so gratful that I wasn't the only female funeral director on staff. There was another girl my age working there, and she had been sexually harassed by him as well. We had a common ground if you will. We spent lots of time together on late-night death calls, so we became friends. What started out as friendship turned into more, and we fell in love. It wasn't long before we got a house together. One day, she asked me to go with her to find crack cocaine. I was outraged. I had no idea she used drugs. What had I gotten myself into. Come with me. I'll show you exactly what I had gotten myself into.

She keeps asking me to try crack. She's pretty relentless with it; so one night, I agree. I figure I'll try it just to get her to shut up. Even after I cave in and try it, that isn't enough. I tell her no more. I don't like it. I'm done. She kept getting it and bringing it home, and I just kept doing it with her. I should have left her, but I didn't, instead I tried to kill myself. I don't remember taking pills, but I remember waking up and feeling like I was going to die and seeing the empty pill bottle on the night stand. What have I done? No, no, this can't be. I don't want to die. I call 911, and I don't remember anything again until I'm being bonded out of jail. I will share with you excerpts from my medical records to fill in the blanks.

"The patient stated she was in the hospital because she OD'd on 100 Zyprexa pills this morning with lemonade. The ambulance brought her in, and when they did, they ran her information and realized that the police had issued a patient hold request because she is wanted as they have been looking for her for writing bad checks for five years. So when she is discharged, the police will take her downtown and put her in jail. The patient stated that she took the pills. The first time I assessed her, she would say a few words and then her eyes would close, and she would continue talking, but it sounded like she was making conversation with someone or answering questions to someone. She was so in and out of consciousness that I mentioned that to her primary doctor, and he stated, 'Well, maybe we should give her some more time.' I said that was fine. When I came back down, Pamela was more coherent although she still would close her eyes and talk as I stated before to someone or answer questions as if somebody else was in the room talking to her. When I asked the patient again how many pills she took, she stated with her eyes closed, 'Two short sleeved ones and a sweatshirt." Her memory recall for remote, recent, and immediate was all poor. Thought content appeared to be delusional, and she continued to talk to somebody.

Although I don't remember, I went to jail that night; and my girlfriend bailed me right out. I was back at work the next day. On the note of the bad checks, I was completely guilty. I wasn't be able to buy diapers or groceries at one point when the girls were very small, so I wrote a check I knew was no good so that I could feed my kids and put pampers on their bottoms. I did what I had to do to survive even if it was illegal. The situation only kept getting worse. She kept bring me crack, and I kept smoking it. I had been late and called off to many times, and I lost my job at the funeral home. We decided to move to a neighboring state and start over. We both got jobs there and finally found an apartment. It was going to be a fresh start, new jobs, new home, no drugs, everything was going to be okay. Until one day, about four months after my last attempt, I can't even tell you what I was thinking or what went wrong. I just don't remember, no matter how hard I try to. It's just a blank. I will share with you again the excerpts from my medical records.

"From the information we can glean with her partner, attempted suicide by taking a handful of prescription medicines they had available for them, and they were also smoking crack cocaine. She was found by the girlfriend's mother that had called and had found that the girlfriend was acting very confused and not making sense on the phone, and when she presented, she found her to be in a confused state, and Pamela was at that point obtuned and not able to answer any questions. She was placed on mechanical ventilation as she is respiratorily unstable. The patient is not responsive to any verbal stimuli, and we are unable to obtain a history and review. Upon admission to the intensive care unit, she was obtunded. She was intubated and not responding except to painful stimuli by withdrawal. Her pupils are minimally if at all reactive. Her core temperature is noted to be 92.6. Heart was tachycardic and had soft systolic murmur. Her CK level [shows damage to the heart muscle] has gone from 216 to 1,682 since admission to the ED. Due to her elevated CK level, it was thought that she may have an early rhabdomyolysis [form of kidney failure] and IV fluids were used vigorously to protect the kidneys. She did have an episode of decreased urinary output and was started on renal dopamine, and it improved. The most worrisome thing is to follow her heart for any arrhythmias to monitor for any seizures."

This is the last attempt I would make to take my own life. I would remain in the intensive care unit for my entire hospital stay of two weeks. I do not remember any of it. I've been told I was very difficult to care for, and I was very combative and childlike while hospitalized. My sister would come up and help bath me because I was so combative. I didn't want anyone touching me. My next memory was of being wheeled out of the hospital and that is foggy. I was taken to the state mental hospital again where I would remain for two weeks. That entire stay is foggy as well. One thing that I do remember about that stay was being punched in the face by a six-foot-tall man. I was on the phone with my kids, and he just walked up and punched me in the face and walked away. Everyone there acted like they didn't see it, including the staff. Beyond that, I have a hard time remembering much about that stay. Because of this whole incident, child services was called; and my girls were placed in the care of my sister until I was released. Yes, I had spiraled out of control to the point my children were taken away from me by the state. I was devastated, but I am a fighter. I am twenty-nine years old.

I was discharged to my parents' home where my children lived with me. I found a job working nights that allowed me to sleep at least six hours, and I attended outpatient rehab and outpatient psychiatric services during the day. This time around, I shared my secret. I finally broke the silence and started opening up. There was so much I couldn't remember; but as I continued on with therapy, I began having flashbacks. I had already been diagnosed with depression, anxiety, bipolar, borderline personality disorder, and now post-traumatic stress disorder. Sometimes, the flashbacks would come in my sleep, sometimes a noise or a smell would trigger them. Certain songs, types of scenery, even seeing types of cars would trigger them. It's like being in the moment that the abuse happened, like I was sucked back in time. Many nights, I woke up fighting for my life, out of breath, sick to my stomach because of what was being revealed to me. I was heavily medicated to treat all these mental disorders I had.

Despite all that, I got my life back together because that's what I do. When I fall down, I get back up, dust myself off, and keep it moving. A few months later, I found a job and a house; and we were back out on our own again. It was a big, beautiful, yellow-with-blue-trim Victorian house. It was previously separated into two apartments but was now converted and opened up into one dwelling. It contained five bedrooms, a living room, dining room with fireplace, and two full bathrooms. The kitchen was located upstairs, large laundry room, and a toy room. It had a fenced in yard and detached two car garage with attached rec room and loft. All it needed was a fresh coat of paint. The funeral home next door owned it. I had left my night job, and I worked for them and lived right next door. I was also a trade embalmer for another company. The facility I used to embalm was located directly across the street from my new home. It was a nice set up.

It wasn't long before I fell in love again. I had met a girl at my previous place of employment, and we were falling in love. My kids got along well with her, and my parents liked her too. It didn't matter that she was ten years younger than me. We often took the kids to an indoor fun park, the movies, and all the fairs in town. It was like we were I big bunch of kids. Food fights at the food court in the mall, long nights of video game playing. We all had a blast together. As time went on, I became depressed again. I was having so many flashbacks and so my medications were increased. I became increasingly depressed and would not get out of bed for hours on end. I had learned from my last hospitalization and all the treatments I was undergoing to reach out for help. I learned a very hard lesson last time, and I vowed not to repeat my past mistakes. I went to the emergency room and asked to be admitted because I didn't feel safe. I was afraid of what I would do to myself. I was admitted to the psychiatric unit for a week stay. The flashbacks continued, and I was having a hard time coping. I promised not try to kill myself ever again, and I was going to keep that promise for my children.

One particular night, I'm lying in bed sleeping when I'm awaken by a flashback. I'm sweating, sick, and lightheaded. I get myself together, and I write about it. That's what I've been taught to do, write it down, get it out. As I am writing, everything starts to get foggy. Now, when I use the term foggy, it's like I am watching myself; and there is fog all around the edges. That's the best way I can explain it. It's as if I am sometimes, next to myself, behind myself, in front of myself, or above myself, watching myself as if I'm in a movie or a dream. I go to the kitchen and retrieve a butcher knife. I take it back to my bedroom and sit on the bed Indian style. I don't want to cut myself; but I can't stop myself. I cut my arm over and over and over again to the point that I required stitches. When I come out of the fog, I realize I need to get help. I can't go on like this. I take myself to the hospital. After my arm is stitched up, I am admitted once again. This time would be a whole new ball game.

Because I was so severely depressed, I was suggested to have electroconvulsive therapy also known as ECT. It is a procedure where I was strapped to a hospital like bed with electrodes placed on my head and placed under general anesthesia through and intravenous line. Small amounts of electric shock were delivered to my brain, and I was then woke up. I underwent several of these treatments while in the hospital and continued having them as an outpatient procedure. I would be in a zombie like state for the rest of the day, and the following day, have no memory of the previous day. What I do remember about these treatments is how I acted when I was waking up from the anesthesia. It's that foggy state I was talking about.

The nurse, she talked to me as if I were a small child, as if she were dealing with a combative, angry, scared little girl. "It's okay, hunny, everything's okay. Now, be a good girl, and drink your juice for me. I'm not going to keep giving you juice if you are going to keep throwing it. If you keep acting like this and don't behave yourself, we are going to stop doing your treatments. Do you understand me?"

Sometimes I would cry. Sometimes I would be scared. Sometimes I would be ready to fight and was very defiant. I believe what they had in front of them was Suzzie, but they didn't understand what was going on. I'm not sure of the number of those treatments I had. My guess is about twenty. This would be the last time I would be hospitalized or have any type of outpatient treatment. I stopped the treatments and got back on my feet. I ended up on disability because of all the treatments; but it wouldn't be for long. We moved out of that big house and into a three bedroom apartment. It was nice and cozy and a good change. The girl I was dating for last three years was increasingly upsetting me with her lack of motivation. She didn't want to work. She wouldn't go back to college, and I was just tired of it. I broke up with her and started to enjoy life again. I dated women because I thought it would be safe. I had been hurt my so many men in my life. I thought it would be different with women. After this relationship, I was done with relationships all together for a while.

One day, I was driving home and blacked out while driving. I woke up to my car going up on a curb, and the tire blowing out. I made a doctor's appointment to get checked out and found out one the psychiatric medications I was taking had caused me to become diabetic. My average blood sugar level over the past three months was over 400. The normal is 74. She wrote me a prescription for a glucometer and test strips. I would have to check my sugars four times a day. She also put me on diabetic medication, and I was gradually taken off the medication that had caused it. I should also mention, I had gained one hundred pounds in the last year, also a side effect of that medication. As I decreased the medication and kept taking the diabetic medication, the weight just started falling off; and I began to feel better. Eventually, I didn't need the diabetic medication anymore. I was getting healthy both physically and mentally. I would need to be for what I was going to face in the near future. I had no idea what my mother had been up to behind my back, but I would soon find out.

While I was in and out of the hospital over the last six months, my mother took it upon herself to help my oldest daughter track down her father. Yes, the father who got me pregnant and left. The father who abused her as a baby. The father who raped her mother. The father who tried to make me believe he was dead so he wouldn't have to pay child support. The father who tried to hit her, her mother, and her unborn sister with a car. Yes, that man. She found him in Texas, and she had been talking to him. I was livid, sick, disgusted. How the hell could you do this? What the fuck were you thinking?

I cannot believe this was happening. I have tried my hardest all her life to keep him away, and my mom goes behind my back and finds this son of a bitch. I was so angry I couldn't see straight and then my daughter came to me and asked me to just give it a chance, so I did, for her.

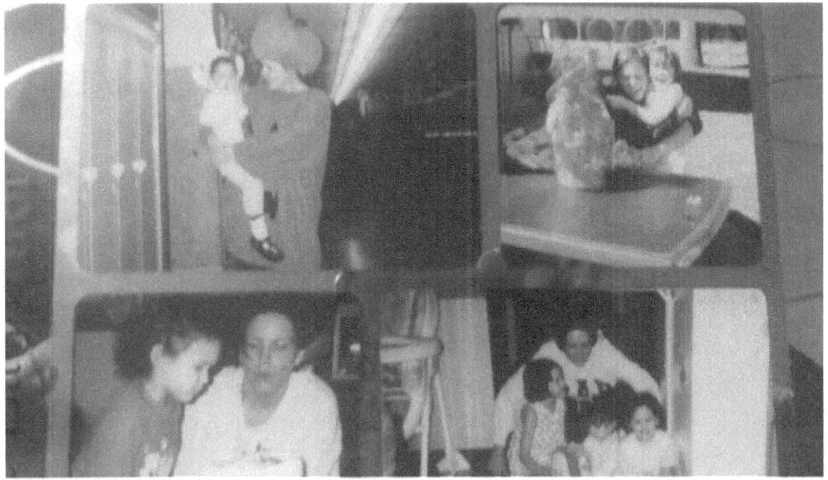

8/00/03 I'm angry ...

8 28 03 I'm in sexual assuld counseling and have been for about 2 and a half mos now Kathy is my counselor. We talked today about my dreams & how they are my past & how they are becoming part of my present reality) & how I must be wanting it & ready for it if im allowing it to happen. I agreed. I talked with her about how I have a hard time believing I was abused even though all the evidence is there. she said its me protecting my self. I have a lot of work to do I want to be whole I want to heal my self. or be healed. I had a dream last night that tics were under my skin & I was sitting on the bath-room counter age 4-6(?) with my legs drawn up my mom standing off to the side my dad standing infront of my tickling the tics from my skin with tweezers he set the tweezers down & the started like touching my private area I decided to close my legs

but he forced them open my mom just stood there watching & looking in the air. I woke up gasping for air. I've had several other nightmares that I have not documented. one in which I just remember a body on top of me hurting me & I woke up screaming get off me & kicking & screaming. I know one thing I cant get down and start feeling sorry for myself but I do have to take care of my self Kathy said to pamper my self a lot.

God

CHAPTER NINE

Queen

My world began changing at a very rapid rate. I broke up with my girlfriend of three years. I found out I would have to have another surgery because my period had gone on for six months. Not only did my daughter start talking to her father, but he moved from Texas back to town. He was married with two children, so I figured he had changed. I did like I was asked of my baby girl and gave him a chance. He seemed to have changed, and his wife was nice. I thought maybe it will be good for her to have them in her life. About the same time all this was happening, I received a job offer that would change my life. I was offered a night position, five at night to eight in the morning, Monday through Friday—no weekends, on-call for a funeral home in a neighboring state. I would only have to work when I received a death call within those hours, and I was paid the same rate no matter how often or not I had to go into work. The position came with paid vacation, paid sick days, a yearly clothing allowance, and paid health insurance. It was perfect for being able to spend time with the kids and who could beat all the perks. I accepted the position and let them know I would be able to start after I had my surgery. It would also require me to move closer to the funeral home. We moved from an apartment to a house, and I had my surgery done. This time, I had and ablation done with the D&C. It's a procedure where they scrape out the uterus and then burn the walls with heated up saline. It took care of the problem for the time being, and I was ready for work.

New job, new home, kids were in better schools right up the street from the house, everything was looking up and then I made one of the worst mistakes of my life. I just didn't realize it at that time, but I would graduate from princess to Queen. Queen of bad decisions that is. I started engaging in a sexual relationship with my oldest daughter's father. Now I had had sex with lots of men who had girlfriends, possibly wives; so it was nothing new for me, and it didn't faze me. He was a great manipulator, and I was easily manipulated. I was still on the heavy side. I had a lot of weight to lose considering. I had maxed out my weight at three hundred twenty pounds. Not to mention, I had not been with a man in seven years. I was easy prey. The affair didn't stop at just him and me. He brought his wife into it as well. I was having sex with both of them. Yes, you read it right. I had absolutely no boundaries whatsoever, but I was raised that way. Just when you think it can't get any worse than me having sex with a man who raped me in the past and then having sex with his wife as well. He convinced his wife to have them all move in with me. It was such a mess. I'm ashamed to even admit, it but it is necessary. I won't get into details only that it happened: and it went on for about a year. It was like an ongoing episode of something you might see on the television, except she didn't know. I mean, I'm pretty sure she knew but could never prove it.

We helped take care of each other kids and the house. We even went and got tattoos together. Yes, I've done some horrible things in my life. I wish I could take back inexcusable things that hurt others, but I can't undo what's done. The thing of it is, it's not in my character to do these things or be like this. I am a warm, loving, optimistic soul who wants to save the world and always have been. I just don't always have control over myself.

I had only been working at the funeral home for about six months when the owner became ill and would be out for a while. My position was changed to working every other weekend and having Wednesdays off. Not what I signed up for, but it was a good job, and I wasn't about to lose it. There were many times that I went without sleep for days on end with this schedule. It is the nature of the business, but I made it work.

It's a Saturday morning, and I have to be at work at eight, and it's a twenty-minute drive. I leave early so I can stop to get gas. When I stop at the gas station and go to get out of the truck, my seat belt won't unbuckle; and I have to climb out of it. I pump my gas and try to get it unbuckled again with no luck. I'm only five minutes away from work. It won't hurt to leave it off. Most of the way is country road anyway. I hop in and head to work. As I come to a stop at a stop sign, the sun is blaring in my eyes, look both ways and proceed on. About halfway through the intersection, I feel the impact of another vehicle; and the next thing I know, I'm flying up, and my SUV is rolled onto the driver's side, and I am sliding down the road. It happened so fast but in slow motion at the same time. By the time my truck stopped, I am pinned between the steering wheel and the caved in windshield. What just happened? I'm alive. I can move everything but my legs. My legs are numb. Then the pain sets in. I lift up my arm to feel my head, and it's hard to breath. I feel glass all over my head. I was hurt but alive. I look around and find my phone. I have to call work. I can't just not show up. The woman who hit me calls 911, and a passerby who happened to be a pastor climbs in the truck and held my hand and prays with me until paramedics arrive. Gas is leaking from the tank being punctured, so they cover me with a heavy fire resistant blanket while they cut the truck open with the Jaws of Life to get me out. As they were pulling me out and placing me on the stretcher, the owner of the funeral home and his brother show up at the scene to check on me. I had three broken ribs and road rash on the entire left side of my body, except for my face and glass embedded in my scalp. Had my seat belt been on, I would not have lived; or I would have been severely brain damaged. It would have been my face and head banging and scraping on the pavement instead of my body. Someone was looking out for me, one of my Angels.

The car accident was around the same my landlords were pressuring me to purchase the house or move out. You see, a few months after I moved in, I started finding suspicious stuff happening. This was before I moved my daughter's father and his family in. I came home from work one day and went down to my bedroom. I noticed my panty drawer was open, and I knew I didn't leave it that way. Upon inspection, I found a couple pair of my underwear missing. I checked the kid's rooms, dirty laundry. I even asked the kids if they were sneaking my underwear. I couldn't explain it and filed it away. Another day, upon arriving home from work, I went down to my room, which was located in the basement as well as the kid's toy room and a bathroom. I walked past the toy room to the bathroom, and I notice a pair of man's boots sitting on the floor next to the Kraft table. There were no men living in my house, and I had never seen these boots before. I'm thinking what the heck is going on here. I ask the kids if they know where the boots came from or if they had seen them before. They had no idea. I was getting creeped out. My oldest daughter's aunt on her father's side, own the car lot kitty corner from our house; so I go pay her a visit. When she told me what she had seen going on at my house, made my jaw drop. She said there was a red pickup parked in front of the house. I said, "Yes, that's my land-lord's husband."

She went on to say she saw him going inside my house while I was a work. She thought I knew. She thought he was fixing things. Oh my god, I couldn't believe it. This pervert was coming in my house, stealing my panties; and what the hell were his boots doing in my kid's toy room. I got in the car and headed over to my landlord's house. I knock on the door, and his wife answered. I explain to her what is happening. Of course, she denies it, and I say, "How do you know your husband's not a pervert and not coming in my house when I'm away? You don't know and suggest you find out what you are dealing with, and tell him to stay the hell away. I have people watching the house and reporting back to me," and I left. Needless to say, they wanted me out; and I didn't want to be there anymore. I stayed for a few more months and found another house, a few min-utes away. By this time, I had let my rapist and his family move in; and we all moved into the new house together.

This did not last much longer. I started dating and stopped all the nonsense with him. He didn't like me dating at all, and that's when I realized it was time for them to go. It only took a couple of months being in the new house, and they were out of there. I felt free. I had lost all that extra weight and was feeling great. I did a lot of internet dating because it allowed me to date from home. I would chat online if I was interested, and the conversation was going good. We would exchange numbers and talk on the phone. If the phone conversation went well, I would meet up and go on a date. I met a few guys, went on a few dates. Some of them I dated briefly; and some of them, I had one-night stands with. There was one guy I talked to a lot. We hit it off great, but he was still married. I told him to come see me when his divorce was final until then we could be friends. There was no way I was going to get involved with a married man again. I learned my lesson. He continued to call and text me; and when his divorce was final, we hooked up. We remained friends with benefits over the years. No strings attached, and I liked it that way.

There was one I guy I met online that I ended up dating and living with for a short period of time. He was eleven years younger than me and honestly, I have no idea what I saw in him. I think it was the sex. Not even that it was great, but he was willing to be risky and do it in public places and frequently at that. What made me break it off with him was he was lazy and unwilling to help me out when I needed it most. I saw him for what he really was, and I didn't need another child to care for.

One day, I started having a lot of back and pelvic pain. I started going to a chiropractor and would feel great after. I left; but a few days later, I was back in pain. One night, it got so bad I could hardly move; so I went to the emergency room where I was treated like a drug seeker. They took a urine sample and drew some blood. When the results came back negative, the doctor asked me what kind of drugs I was looking for, to which I replied, "No kind. I want you to figure out what is wrong with me. I'm not having this pain for no reason. He basically dismissed me, wrote me a prescription for nonnarcotic pain medication, and sent me on my way. What a jerk. A few weeks went by and the pain was only getting worse, so I called to make an appointment with my general practitioner. She was on vacation, so I was scheduled with another doctor. I didn't care. I had to figure out what was going on with my body.

I arrive at the doctor's office, check in, and have a seat in the waiting area. A few minutes later, the nurse calls me back. She takes my weight, blood pressure, and checks my temperature. We discuss my symptoms, and she decides I should have a pelvic exam. She leaves me the gown and sheet and says she will be back with the doctor in a few minutes. She returns in just a few minutes as promised with the doctor, and it's a man. I've had female doctors all of my adulthood with the exception of my obstetricians because I am uncomfortable with men and rightly so. I assure myself the nurse is in here, and it will be over fast. I place my legs in the stirrups and skootch my butt down to the end of the table as instructed. As the doctor goes to do the digital vaginal examination, he placed his fingers on my clitoris and moved them around in a circular motion, at the same time, he said, "I found the button. Now I can slide right in." I can't believe what is happening to me. What did he just say? What did he just do? I look at the nurse, and she is looking shocked as well. I was just sexually assaulted by a doctor. Guess what I did about it? Nothing, I did nothing. I can't believe I did nothing. Do you hear me? I was sexually assaulted by a doctor, and I did absolutely nothing about it. You know why? Because I was trained all my life to do nothing about it. I felt like I had become the poster child for sexual assault as if I had it tattooed across my forehead. It's saddening and sickening at the same time. After he assaults me, he then tells me he doesn't feel anything wrong. Maybe I'm constipated. Go home a take laxatives for a few days; and if it's not better, we will get an x-ray.

A few more days go by, and I'm all cleaned out but still in all this pain. I go in and get my x-rays done. A few days later, the nurse calls me and says she is scheduling me for an abdominal cat scan because it's recommended by the radiologist from the x-ray results. Finally, we are getting somewhere. A few days later, I get a disturbing call from my physician. She is referring me to a gynecologist because the cat scan showed tumors in my uterus. Of course, I had a lot of questions that she couldn't answer; so I had to wait. After the gynecologist saw me, he had me stay to do an ultrasound of my uterus.

That is when he found that my uterus, that had been scraped and burned clean two years prior, had been invaded by tumors. They were so large they were popping my spine out of place, causing all my back pain. He then informed me I would have to have a hysterectomy. He put me on pain medication and scheduled me for a biopsy. I was terrified. When I went in for my biopsy, I had no idea it would be so painful; but it was. It made me cry. After the biopsy, I met with the scheduling nurse and was all set for surgery the following month. If the biopsy came back as cancerous, they would do it sooner. Fortunately, it was benign. Now, the wait until surgery.

You would think I would be a pro at going under anesthesia having six surgeries, a C-section, and numerous ECT treatments; but something happened during my last ECT treatment that made me terrified. I believe this incident is what made me stop the treatments coupled with the fact that they were having to start IVs in my feet. I am all strapped down to the table, electrodes on my head when they start to put me under. This time is different than every other time because I'm still awake; but I can't breathe, and I can't communicate to them that I'm still awake. I'm screaming in my head, trying to move my hand so they will see I'm awake. They can't shock me while I'm awake. I'm going to die. I can't breathe. I can't breath and then I was gone. Ever since that episode, I became terrified of being put under.

My surgery date is here, and all goes well. My uterus was so enlarged they had to remove it by cesarean. They removed one ovary that was effected but were able to leave the other. That meant no hormones or menopause for me. Before my procedure, I asked the doctor if he would save my uterus so that I could see it. He told me he couldn't, but he could take pictures for me. What a great idea! I figured it's my uterus. I should be able to see it before they throw it in the trash. My stay in the hospital was only a couple of days, but I would be off work for six weeks. I was recovering well for the first few days then one morning I woke up with a fever. After having a fever for a couple of days, I called the doctor. He had me go to the hospital for a chest x-ray. It showed I had pneumonia. I was put on antibiotics and had to follow up with him in a week for staple removal, so he would follow up on the pneumonia as well.

At my follow-up appointment, my lungs sounded clear; and I was feeling much better. Now to get the staples out. I pull my shirt up and my pants down to my hips to expose the incision. I get up on the table and lie back. This isn't my first time having this done, so I know its easy breezy. First staple pulled a little uncomfortable. Second, the same. Third, I'm screaming out in pain. What the hell are you doing to me? It's not supposed to hurt like this. Fourth staple, I'm crying. The skin had grown over the staples, so they were pinching pieces of skin off when pulling the staples, and I had to lie there and take it for twelve staples. I cried and cringed the whole time. You should have seen the looks I got when I walked out of the examining room into the waiting room. I'm sure it sounded like I was being tortured; and well, I really was. About four months go by, I recovered well and was back into my normal routine or so I thought. Everyone was all tucked in bed; and when I lay down to sleep, I just couldn't fall asleep. It then escalated to being restless, so I watched TV for a while and then I just couldn't sit still. I got up and paced the house all night. I was having an anxiety attack. I couldn't even get myself into the car to drive to the hospital, so I paced the house all night. Finally, when the sun started to come up, I managed to drive to my parent's house where my sister was living at that time. I woke her, and she drove me to the emergency room where I was treated with the utmost respect and received excellent care. The nurse explained to me that my hormones weren't working correctly after the hysterectomy. They gave me medicine to calm me down and had me schedule a doctor's appointment. A few days later, I started having the same pain I was having before the hysterectomy and went back to the ER. After another ultrasound, I was told the ovary that was left was now riddled with tumors. It quit working. That was why I had the anxiety attack. My hormones were brought to an abrupt halt. I was put on a few different medications to try to shrink the tumors, but they only grew larger. This meant another surgery. This surgery was to be simpler, less invasive. It was one ovary, and they were going to remove it vaginally.

Now, this is where I told my boyfriend to hit the road. He had been absolutely no help to me after my last surgery, and I wasn't going to deal with it again. I broke it off and sent him packing. My sister went with me the day of my surgery. I was to be done in an hour. When three hours had gone by, she was worried and went up to the desk to ask what was going on. She was informed the surgery had become complicated. They to cut me open again, and it would be another hour and a half before they were done.

A one-hour surgery turned into four and a half hours. When they closed me up, this time, they used internal sutures, glue, and steri strips, no staples. What was supposed to be two weeks off work turned into another six weeks off. I was started on hormone replacement therapy and antidepressants because the hormone change was hard to deal with. In regular menopause, the hormones are depleted over time. With surgical menopause, they are depleted immediately. You want to talk about feeling crazy. I hadn't felt this crazy in a few years, and I didn't like it at all. I was eventually put on hormones that worked well for me, and I felt much better. I had bigger problems than my hormones though.

One night, my middle daughter and I were coming home. As we pulled into our cul-du-sac, I noticed the police parked in front of our house, and they were knocking on our door. Instead of pulling in my driveway, I pull in front of a neighbor's house on the other side of the cul-du-sac and park. I instruct my twelve-year-old to get down in the seat, and we waited until they left, backed up, and pulled in our garage. They returned again at two in the morning and I couldn't hear them banging on my door. My room was in the basement and couldn't hear it. The same daughter that was in the car with me, opened the door. When the police asked for me, she told them I was sleeping, shut the door, and locked it. All the girls slept downstairs with me ask the police continued to knock. We turned the TV up and fell back to sleep.

The next day, I went to the courthouse and filed a motion to vacate the warrant they were trying to arrest me for. I had missed a court date at least ten years prior for a bill I didn't pay. I took that motion to vacate and hung it on my front door; so when the police came back for me, they would see it and leave me alone. It worked. I went to court and cleaned my old mess up. I didn't remember missing court. I didn't even remember the circumstances that put me there. So you can imagine my surprise when only a month later, I was pulled over for not wearing my seatbelt a block away from my house, and I was arrested.

When I tell you have giant gaping holes in my past, I am not exaggerating. I thought I was being arrested for the same warrant I had just cleared up, but I found out it was something totally different. Something else I couldn't remember I had done. But wait, it gets better. They search my car and find a glass bowl in my purse. There wasn't any weed in it, but they still charged me with it. Because I was being charged with drug possession, I got the privilege of being strip searched at the jail. That was humiliating, to say the least. My sister came and bailed me out. I never told anyone that I couldn't remember what had happened to get me the warrant. I was too embarrassed. By this time in my life, I was used to covering up for myself. I was becoming used to cleaning up after myself even if I didn't know where the mess came from. There was one other time that I was arrested. I believe it was in the same year as these two incidents. I was pulled over for a reason I don't remember. I had my youngest daughter in the car. They came back to my car after running my license and asked me to step out of the car. I was under arrest. They let me call my mom to come get my daughter before they took me away. Someone bailed me out. I don't remember who.

Over the past six months, I had two major surgeries causing me to be out of work for four months and had to pay bail on two separate occasions. I wasn't making ends meet and received an eviction notice. Now, I had to figure out where we were going to live. I simply didn't have the money to move or even pay my bills. Unfortunately, this was something I was used to. I never had help from the kids' fathers, but I always figured it out. There were many times we went without heat, electric, and sometimes even water; but we were never homeless. I was in need of a miracle, and it's a good thing I believed in them. I put a call out to my angels, asking them for a much needed miracle; and they delivered just a few days later. As I opened the mail, to my surprise, there was a check for twenty-five thousand dollars. Apparently, when I was on disability, I was under paid the entire two years; and they sent me a check to compensate me. My angels had answered my prayers. The first thing I did was repay my parents for all the help they had given me over the years then I found a nice house in a better neighborhood for my children. We were starting over again, and that was okay because we were moving in a forward direction. One of my mottos is "I don't move backward," unless it's only a step in which I use to observe the situation to help me get a clearer perspective. I've always raised the girls to know that they can accomplish anything they put their minds to. The saying "I can't" was illegal in our house. I lived by that. I tried to show my girls that anything was possible no matter what the odds. I was never a model mother. I failed my children time and again. I put them through things children should never have to go through, but I tried with what I had and what I knew. I stayed up through the nights when they were newborns and cared for them single handedly. I taught them to crawl, walk, and run. I potty trained them and kissed their boo-boos all better. I taught them to love each other even when they didn't see eye to eye. At bedtime, I read stories and rubbed their backs to sleep. I nurtured them back to health when they were sick. I taught them right from wrong and have gone to bat for them every time it was needed. I love nothing more in this world than my beautiful girls. They are my world. I would, without question, give my life for each of them at any given moment. They are my pride and my joy, my inspiration and my motivation. They are the reason I still walk this earth today. They are my angels. I cannot deny that I have been the queen of bad decisions all my life, but I am slowly but surely changing that with them as my motivation.

CHAPTER TEN

Thunderstorms and Rainbows

We got all settled in our new home. I never minded moving because I love decorating a new space. It's like painting on a blank canvas, creating a work of art. I've often entertained the idea of having my own interior decorating business; and maybe someday, I will. Now let me tell you, we had a blast at this house. My home was always the home where all the kids came to. I was mom to not only my children but many of their friends as well. I mothered them all, fed them, gave them advice, and many of them a place to stay. We had New Year's Eve parties that turned the kitchen into a dance floor. I even started up a ladies' night out in my garage. I had a double long garage, so the back half was set up with couches, a pool table, a fireplace, and a card table. We had a blast out there.

One night, a friend of mine and I decided to go out to shoot some pool. We were hanging out and having a good time when a gentleman approached us and started up conversation. To make a long story short, I left with his number. I waited a few days to text him, and then we talked for a while before going out on a date. He wasn't the only one I was talking to, but he stood out the most; and after a few weeks, we were hot and heavy. He was talking about taking me to Vegas for a weekend getaway and all this wonderful stuff.

One day, I got a call at work from my mom. She was at my house when an officer came looking for me. He had a check in his hand that was mine, but it wasn't my handwriting on it and not my signature. This man I was dating had stolen a check from me, wrote it out for $250 to rent a backhoe. After he rented it, he took it and sold it to someone for twenty-five hundred dollars; and he tried to make it look like I had a hand in it. Does my luck ever get better? I had to go to the rental place with the police so the owner could verify I wasn't the woman with him passing the check and stealing from him. What a mess. After that, I swore off relationships. I was single and ready to mingle; and to top it off, I was going to write about it and share it with the world. I was on a mission to write a book all right, "The Little Pink Book." Men had their little black books of naughtiness, so I was going to write one for the ladies. In order to write, I had to do research; so I set out on a mission to collect as many numbers as I could get and conquer as many penises as I could. Yes, I said it; and yes, I did it. One day, I will write all about it in great detail. For now, I will share a couple of my rendezvous with you.

I was doing a lot of internet dating, but it wasn't panning out. One of my friends was always hosting parties, and they were always a great time. This particular night, I was introduced to a tall light and handsome man. Now, I could tell from talking to him, he wasn't dating material; but I figured he might be good for a ride or two, if you know what I'm saying. We talked for a while, but I could tell he was just a player. It was my birthday and a bunch of us girls decided to go out and let loose. That's exactly what we did. The drinks were flowing, and the dance floor was my friend. Toward the end of the night, I got that text. You know that bar-close booty-call text. I was much too intoxicated to drive, so I had my girls drop me off at this guy's apartment after we left the bar. He's talking in my ear about birthday sex and all that jazz when I simply say, "I'm too drunk to have sex with you, and if you are a real gentleman, you will just let me sleep," and he did. He even got up the next morning and drove me to my car. A few days later, I figured I would reward him for being such a gentleman. Big mistake, he was the one of the worst lays I had ever had, and that was the end of that.

Valentine's Day is a couple of weeks after my birthday, and my fun loving friend was hosting a Valentine's Day party, and I was there. We had a great time that night. Little did I know, there was a guy there that had his eye on me the entire time, but I wouldn't find out until a few days later when I received a call from my friend. I don't exactly remember how it was stated to me, but I was shocked. She invited me over to hang out one evening with her, her husband, and her husband's brother. Now her brother-in-law was also her ex-boyfriend, long story; and it's hers to tell. In our conversation she let me know that her brother-in-law was interested in hooking up with me. I was like, this is your ex, what are you talking about? She said she didn't care. They were cool like that and so on. My friends, and I had a habit of sharing men. There had been a few times I got out my little pink book and gave my friends numbers in their time of need. I took this as that and accepted her invitation to hang out and see where it went.

The day had come, and I was ready. My hair freshly colored red of course. My body was bronzed from tanning, and I was looking and feeling amazing. As I was waiting for my friend to call to give me the thumbs up to come over, as I was waiting anxiously, I received a call from my friend Camilia. She invited me over to hang out while I was waiting to get my call. She said it would ease my mind to come hang out and not just be sitting around waiting. She was right, and I knew it, so I headed on over to a mutual friend of ours house where everyone was hanging out. Little did I know, this spur of the moment decision was part of my destiny in the making. When I walked in the house, everyone was seated in the living room watching a movie, so I joined having a seat on the couch. There was someone there I had never met before. Let's call him tall, dark, and sexy, can I. Even though I was on my way to a hot date, I took notice. After all, I was working on my book and wasn't counting any encounter out. We all sat and watched the movie. When it was over, I stepped out to smoke a cigarette. The next thing I knew, this beautiful man was joining me; and we struck up a conversation. A few minutes later, I got that text message I was waiting for. It was go time, and off I went. Now I won't get into too much detail about that night, but what I will share is that it involved a bottle of patron tequila, a hotel room, and an entire twelve count box of magnum XL condoms. Oh yes, it was so fun. I left without my shoes and didn't even notice until he called and told me.

The next day, my friend Camila called to see how my night had gone. She mentioned to me that handsome man I had met at our friend's house was a fan of the big booty club of which I am a member. "Perfect, give him my number," I told her, "I'm on a roll. Let's not stop the momentum."

It was only a couple of hours after I gave her the okay to pass my number, on that, I received a call from Mr. Wonderful. We talked for hours; and when I say hours, I mean twelve hours straight. We had so much in common. Even two of our children had the same names. It was as if we were living in parallel universes, and they finally collided. He came to visit me the very next day, and it was an instant attraction, but I made him wait for sex because I didn't want to come off as easy or a whore. Too funny, I made him wait until the next day. After that, we were inseparable and falling in love. The sex was phenomenal, earthshaking, and magnificent just to name a few adjectives. That wasn't it though, he was soft but masculine, loving but firm. He mirrored me but walked to his own beat. I fell hard and fast for this eloquent man. It wasn't long before I moved into his house and made it a home. This was temporary, as I was waiting for my parents to move out of their home; and I was going to pay them rent and eventually purchase the house. In the meantime, we spent as much time as possible together. I have to admit there were red flags from the beginning; and truthfully speaking, I should have dismissed the relationship from the beginning, but I chose to stay. Although he had separated from his ex and had his own place, there were the children; and they were used to fullest extent as a manipulation by his ex. It was clear to me that I was going to have to fight to keep my man, part of which required me to turn my head to what was going on. I knew what I was dealing with and chose to stay in the relationship. After all, I had watched my mom turn her head to so many situations to keep her man, so I was trained well. Deep in my heart, I knew that he just needed time to separate himself from this other woman, the mother of his children, so I hung in there.

I was out running errands one afternoon when I received a phone call from Camilia. She called to let me know my man was indeed leading a double life and was still carrying on a relationship with his ex behind my back. Just how did she know? He had confided in her boyfriend, and he in return told her. I knew he was cheating on me with her, so I started looking for clues; and sure as shit, I found what I was looking for.

One day, he told me some lie about where he was going; and I had figured out where his ex lived. When I went over to her house, there was his car parked outside. I had the code to unlock the car and pop the trunk, so I did that and wrote fuck you on a cd he had made me and placed it on the driver's seat. I then texted him and told him to go check his car. After that, I went home and packed all his things and told him to come get them. When he came to get his things, we talked and decided to stay together. Yes, I stayed with this man who didn't really love me, and I'm not sure why, but I did. Maybe it was because we had just moved into a new home together. Maybe it was because I knew deep down in my heart, he really did love me. Maybe it was because I just wanted to be loved even if I didn't know what love really looked like.

It was coming up on a year of our relationship, and I still had not met his kids, so I put a bug in one of his friend's ears. I told her I was going to kick him out and end the relationship if he didn't bring his kids around. I wasn't putting up with anymore. A few days later, when he went to pick them up for a visit and to my surprise, he brought them to the house to introduce them to me. I won't lie, I fell in love them instantly. From then on, they came every weekend; and I gave it my all to make them feel comfortable. We played together. I read them bedtime stories. I treated them like my own and loved them like my own. This was the first time I had dated anyone with kids, but I knew how to care for children. You can ask anyone I know. I have the biggest heart, and I shared it. I shared it even when I knew he had not stopped the relationship with his ex. I shared it even when he treated me badly because of this. I shared my love despite my pain. I just kept fighting because that's what I do. I fight for what

I believe in even when it seems like an uphill battle. I keep it moving. I keep pushing through. I find the silver lining.

You have to be wondering why I stayed. I stayed because it wasn't all bad, not by any means. This man looked out for my well-being aside from cheating. We were living in my parent's home, but renting it. They would stop by without notice, hold family meetings with my sister and children at our home without us knowing while we were at work. He sat me down and explained to me that what was going on was not right and that I had trouble making boundaries. He also suggested I make a counseling appointment because my father stopping by every week was disturbing me greatly. He also agreed to help me stand up to my father. The next time he popped by, I decided to tell my dad that it was inappropriate and that I needed notice before a visit. I was terrified at the thought of even doing this, but I did it. It wasn't long before my father stopped on by with no notice, and John gave me the strength to stand up to him. I wanted to do it on my own, so John stood in the hallway and waited for me to start talking. Well, needless to say, good old dad didn't like what I had to say and refused to take a seat when I asked him to. John walked by the living room where we were, and my dad changed his mind and sat down. I said what I had to say, and he got up to leave. While we were in the driveway, my dad confronted me about some blinds hanging in the house that I had changed, and I told him I replaced them. He came toward me like when I was little, like he was going to backhand me. He was on his way to strike me, and John stepped out of the house into his view. He abruptly turned around and went back to his car. This would be the first time anyone had defended me from my father, and this would be the last time I would see or talk to my father.

A few months later, my parents showed up uninvited and unexpectedly when they knew I was at work, and John would be home alone. They were anything but nice to him. During the visit, my dad told john we wouldn't be living there in a few months anyway. John immediately called me at work to tell me what had happened. I, in turn, called my mom and confronted her. Her reply was to call me back in a few minutes. When she called back, she told me that my dad was just angry and didn't mean what he said. I had had it! I was done putting up with their crap, and I told her so, no more intruding! I know you are wondering, after all these people did to harm me in life, what was I doing still having a relationship with them. Better yet, how could I possibly trust them. I would soon find out exactly how evil my father was, as if I didn't already have enough proof. I am thirty-nine years old.

A couple of years had gone by since we moved into the house, and I decided to surprise my man for his birthday with a trip to Jamaica. We had an amazing time there. It was absolutely serene and beautiful. When we returned, we started making preparations to buy the house. The following month, I let my mom know we would soon be ready to buy the house. I was so excited! My excitement would quickly turn to dismay. A couple of weeks later, I received an eviction notice.

Now let me put things into perspective for you. It's winter. It's a month from my birthday. We were getting ready to purchase the house, and I get an eviction notice. What the hell is going on? Well, I would have to figure that out on my own; and indeed, I did. We found a place to live, a bigger, better house. A house that didn't contain so many horrible memories. It would be only a few short days after we moved that I would find out the level of betrayal my parents were capable of. I was evicted from my home because they had let the house go into foreclosure. I had been giving them money for a house payment they weren't even making. But wait, it gets even better. They offered my eldest daughter to live there for the price of utilities. When she said she would have a hard time affording it, they suggested she have her father move in with her. Yes, the man who abused her, the man who raped me, the man who manipulated me into all kinds of craziness, the man my parents hated because of what a horrible person he was. My daughter agreed and moved that man into my parents' house. Before it became official, my sister told my parents, "If you do this, you will never have a chance of reconciling your relationship with her."

They didn't care. You see, they had manipulated my children and turned them against me. They had them keeping tabs on me and reporting back to them, and they were talking badly about me to my own children. They had already taken away my innocence, my mental health, and my home. Now, they were trying to take my kids; and they had already turned my sister against me. I completely lost my shit. I sat down and wrote my mom, my dad, and my sister very lengthy letters. I didn't hold back. I told my parents that I wasn't crazy. I was mentally ill because of the torture they subjected me to growing up. I told them about how much I hated them for all the abuse and for never really loving me. Page after page of anger, rage, and hate represented year after year of physical, sexual, emotional, and mental abuse. I finished it off by letting them know, if I ever found out that my children were hurt by my father, I would be there to kill them both; and I hoped they had a terribly hard time sleeping at night.

In my letter to my sister, the key thing I remember is talking to her about getting counseling. I always talked to my sister about getting help, help to deal with everything we went through; but I also knew I couldn't push her into it. These people called our parents were wolves in sheep's clothing; and in order to have any kind of *normal* life after being raised by them, required years of counseling.

I placed each of those handwritten letters in their own manila envelopes and labeled them with each of their names. I drove over to that house and placed them in the mailbox; and in that moment, I felt a weight lifted from my burdened shoulders. The only regret I have about writing and delivering the letters is that I didn't make copies of the letters, and I don't remember most of what I wrote. I would have loved to share them with you. All hope is not lost. My mom tends to keep things. Maybe one day when she passes, I'll find them in her belongings.

We had just moved into the new house and were settling in, but something wasn't right with my boyfriend. He was acting very erratic, not sleeping, being very edgy, having racing thoughts. It was frightening me. It got worse over a couple of days, to the point where he seemed like an entirely different person who had no control over himself. I tried to get him to a hospital, but he wouldn't go. I didn't know what to do, so I called everyone I could think of to come help.

He held a friend of his at gunpoint in the basement. His friend was able to talk him down and escape. My husband then came to the kitchen and retrieved the knives and chased people out of the house with them. He also asked to his mom and his aunt. He knew something was wrong but wouldn't get help. It escalated to a point where we all to flee our home and leave him there losing his mind. It just wasn't safe. We had no idea what he was capable of. He had knives out on the counter and had threatened a couple of people. I took the kids to a hotel and tried to think about what to do. While I had a moment to breathe, I reflected on the situation and realized how well I had handled it. Then I realized, I had been trained all my life how to handle situations like this. My father was a rageaholic, so I was used to switching into survival mode. A couple of hours had gone by when I received a call from his sister telling me she had to call 911. They gained entrance into the home and arrested him. When I returned back home, I was faced with belongings all over the yard, repairs to be made to our new home, and just a big mess to clean up. Not only was I facing this mess, my boyfriend was in jail on multiple charges with a high bond; and what the hell happened.

It took me a couple of weeks, but I bonded him out, and I already made a doctor's appointment for him. He was diagnosed with bipolar disorder, having a manic episode and was placed on medication. He was still manic when he got home, and it was rough road until I got him into a psychiatrist, and he was placed on medication for bipolar disorder, and he was also diagnosed with posttraumatic stress disorder. You see, my boyfriend has own story as well. It's not my story to tell. I only hope that one day, he will find the strength and courage to share it through his healing process. Now I'd like to think that you wouldn't believe what happened next; but knowing my history, I'm sure you won't be surprised.

He asked me to marry him, and I accepted. We were married a few weeks later, in our home, with just a few people present. The kids were not even invited because of the damage my parents were doing. They were lying to my children, manipulating them, and continuing to turn them against me. My hands were tied. I felt horrible, but it was just how it had to be. We promised to have a wedding with everyone present in the future when things died down and emotions settled.

Speaking on settling emotions, it didn't seem like it was going to happen. After talking it over with my husband, we decided it was time the kids new about my past. I did not give them gory details, only that my sister and I were physically and sexually abused by their grandfather. I couldn't let them go on idolizing a monster. They needed to know the truth. Guess what, they didn't believe me. They took the information I gave them and ran to my mother with it. I got a text from her saying she talked to my dad, and he said he would never do something like that. I was obviously easily brainwashed by my husband and counselors because I was mentally ill. Unbelievable, but is it really? No, it's not that unbelievable in all reality. My heart was broken. Broken because my mom was still making excuses for my father, broken into tiny pieces because she was lying to my children to protect my father, and crushed because my own children believed them over me. If it weren't for my husband standing by my side, encouraging me, supporting me, and holding me tight when I needed it the most, I would have gone out of my mind once again. Even though all this was going on, we found happiness in each other. We often refer to ourselves as a power couple who can accomplish anything we put our minds to. Individually, we are amazing people; but together, we are phenomenal! We knew that everything that was going on with our children would pass eventually, and our relationships would heal.

It wasn't long before our intuition would prove right. We found out our eldest daughter was pregnant and having a baby girl. Aside from having my children, this had to be the happiest day of my life! The news was indeed repairing our relationship with our children. She had moved out of my parents' house only after kicking her father out a few months prior. I knew if I sat back and waited, it would all work itself out. Yes, I am a firm believer that absolutely everything happens for a reason. We started planning the baby shower. I even got to be present for an ultrasound. It's a girl! During the ultrasound, she turned her head and looked at us. It was amazing! I'm going to be a grandma. GG would be my name! I had my relationship back with my daughters. I had my first granddaughter on the way. My husband and I were grooving right along.

It was also around this time that my older brother, who I had never met, came to visit us. We had been in contact off and on over social media for a couple of years. During one of our online conversations, I told him, "I know that I don't know you, but I want you to know that I love you because you are my brother, and I'm so happy to have you in my life."

So yes, he came and visited us; and it felt wonderful. All these years and I finally got to hug my brother. I got meet him and know him. What could be better than that? I'll tell you what was better than that; meeting me and hearing my story eased his burden and helped him heal a little and be less angry.

You see, all these years, he had held on to this anger of our father leaving him. In his eyes, he left and moved on and gave his all to his new family. When I told him about my life experiences with this man being my father, he realized that it was actually a blessing that he left. He expressed heartfelt sorrow for all that I had endured, but it lightened his spirit and took his anger away. Knowing that I could change his outlook and help him with my story was the best gift he could give me. We had a great time getting to know each other. It was a great beginning to our new relationship.

I had yet to repair my relationship with my sister and mother, but I knew in time it would come. It came sooner than I had expected. It came when tragedy struck our family. My daughter had a doctor's appointment one afternoon, a routine visit as she was five months along. She usually called me after to tell me how it went, and we would talk all about baby and baby things for a while. When she called me this time to tell all about her visit, it was to inform me the baby had died, and she had to go deliver her stillborn not tomorrow but the day after. This was absolutely not happening. It couldn't be. I couldn't grasp it. My heart broke into a million pieces. The pain was unbearable. The best way to explain it to you is like this. It was more intense than absolutely anything I had endured in my entire life, gut-wrenching, agonizing, torturous pain; and it wasn't because of the loss I was feeling. It was because I couldn't take this horrible pain away from my baby girl. There was absolutely nothing I could do to ease her pain, nothing. When she was little, I could kiss the pain away, rub her head and run my fingers through her hair when she was upset. I could take my fingers and trace her face to calm her down. I could still do all those things, but they wouldn't bring her baby back. Her baby girl was dead, and I couldn't fix it for her. I couldn't wake her up from this nightmare and hold her and tell her it was just a bad dream. You want to talk about being brought crashing down to your knees. This is exactly what will do it. I knew the only thing I could do for my baby was to carry her through this storm, and that is exactly what I did.

Today is the day. The day we have to come to terms with this nightmare. There is no way around it, over it, or under it. We just have to walk through this storm one small step at a time. We arrive at the hospital; and as we are walking in, my baby girl says to me, "I don't want to do this, Momma."

I replied to her, "I know you don't, baby girl, but we just have to. I am right here with you the whole way. I am your strength right now."

I coached her through that delivery like I had so many women before her, but with so much more. When she was born, the reality hit hard. There was silence, and all hope was lost. We had still been praying for a miracle, one we would not receive. Family and friends still all came up to the hospital to visit. I suggested she involved those who loved and cared for her, and she agreed. The love and support in that hospital room was what absolutely beautiful. It almost made us forget we were there to say goodbye instead of hello. I stayed as long as my daughter would allow me to. I held and rocked my grand-daughter. I kissed her and admired how beautiful she was. I soaked as much up as I could because I knew this was all I would get.

Because I am a funeral director, when it was time for my daughter to be released, I was allowed to take my granddaughter into my care at our funeral home. I wrapped her up in a blanket, and my sister and I exited the hospital with her. I drove while my sister held her niece in her arms on the long ride to the funeral home. I had to take my first born granddaughter and place her in a cooler, shut the door, and leave her there until the next day when I would have to dress her for her funeral service. Because she was so small, I went shopping for her funeral attire in the doll section at a local store. As I am standing in the checkout lane, the woman behind me tries to make conversation with me about the dresses I had picked out. I tried ignoring her, but she kept asking me questions about the dresses and what dolls did I use them for, and I finally broke down. I said, "These dresses are for my dead granddaughter's funeral service," and I just started crying right there in the checkout lane right in front of everyone. You know what, I was not okay; but I was okay with it. I quickly pulled myself together as I had been trained to all my life, paid for my dresses and left the store. I took the dresses to my daughter so she could pick. I took her choice of dresses and headed to the funeral home to dress my granddaughter for her funeral service the next day. The funeral took place at the funeral home, and burial was to be the next morning. I would see my mom for the first time in two years and my father. Well, he didn't show up. He also didn't show up for my middle daughter's graduation, which was the same day as my granddaughter's burial. His excuse was he was sick, but he managed to come to town on other occasions. My children fell for his act, but I didn't; and you want to know what, I was gratful he didn't show up.

It would be the following year that he would finally die. When I found out he had become ill and was placed on hospice, it was all I could do to keep myself from paying him a visit. A visit where I fantasized about shutting the bedroom door, being in the room alone with him, climbing on top of his weak frail body, and suffocating him with a pillow until he just stopped living. I could have very easily did it and got away with it, but I didn't go to see him until he died. The only reason I went is because my children loved him. I did it for them and only them. I had been wishing my father dead and waiting for him to die since I was a small child. I never shed a single tear when he died, not at the funeral arrangements or the funeral service.

A couple of months before my father passing, we found out that my youngest daughter was pregnant. Not only was she having a baby so was my eldest. It was her second chance after the death of her first. This time, she was cautious to protect her feelings; and it's a good thing she did. At three months, she had a miscarriage. It was exactly one year to the date that she had lost the first baby to still birth. I accompanied her to the hospital for her D and C, and I stayed the night with her at the hospital to care for her. I just couldn't bring myself to leave her side. Her pain was unbearable even though she acted brave. I knew she was crumbling on the inside. Sometimes, the only thing you can do as a parent to help your children is to be present. Sometimes that's all they need. This is not only true of parenting relationships but all relationships especially with marital partners. We have to be present with each other, and here is where my husband and I created our next thunderstorm.

After the death of my first granddaughter, my father passing, and the loss of another grandbaby, I completely shut down. I absolutely could not handle it all emotionally, and I did what I had been trained to do, and shut the emotion off. When I was growing up, I was not allowed to show emotion. I wasn't allowed to cry or even think about crying. I wasn't allowed to get angry, be angry, or express my anger in any way shape or form. I swallowed it all and started to shove it all down deep inside. I turned to my husband for support and told him that we would need him now more than ever because all these things were happening to me, and I was noticing them. I knew I had to do something different this time and talk. But no matter how I approached it, we would just argue all of the time. I took on a second job to fill my time, and I coasted on auto pilot. My husband and I argued all the time. He stopped taking his medication properly and was pretty much living in a state of mania. It got so bad that I was sneaking his pills in his coffee whenever I could. I knew he was having an affair, but I couldn't prove it, and he sure wasn't going to admit it. Trust me, I tried. I felt so defeated. All this loss, and now my husband had turned his back on me too.

The storm wasn't even near over. It only picked up momentum and turned into a category F5 tornado. One day, my husband came home from a psychiatry appointment and informed me his doctor was taking him off his medications. She said she didn't think he needed them. My response was, "Are you fucking kidding me?

She obviously doesn't know what she is talking about. She doesn't live with you."

It just got worse and worse; the harder I tried to fix the situation, the more it became broken. Instead of taking his medications, he started drinking alcohol. He was having an affair—to the point he chose to spend time with his mistress instead of supporting me on the day of my father's funeral. He wasn't helping me out financially anymore to the point we were living in a house without electricity. It was a nightmare of a situation. Christmas came and went as did New Year's, and it almost seemed for a while that things were getting better. I attributed it to the fact that I had been getting his medications in him via coffee for a month straight. He brought me flowers for Valentine's Day and popped up at the office with flowers one day as a surprise. He was really trying, but I didn't give that back. I stayed stuck. I couldn't move forward without acknowledging the past. His drinking became an all the time thing; and soon, he started rearranging our two story, five bedroom, three car garage home. When I say rearranging, I mean it looked like a tornado tore through it, picked shit up and threw it back in different places all over the house. As I looked around in complete and utter dismay, this was an all too familiar scene to me. What my husband had created was what was going on in his head. I understood it because what I stood in the middle of was like a map of my own mind. I had to make several calls to the police and had them over to our home several times until one day, he gave them a reason to take him with and get him some help. I left the home and stayed at friend's house. His behavior was so unpredictable. I had no choice. I was awoken the next morning to a phone call where he said to me, "Bitch, I set your house on fire."

I called 911 and headed home. Fortunately, the fire was on the back porch; but the contents of our home were in even more disarray that when I left. He was admitted to the hospital, and I was his enemy. He was divorcing me, and we were over.

I did the only thing I knew how to do. I did what I had been doing all my life. I started picking up the pieces with the hope that he would come back to reality when stabilized on medications. He was released from the hospital after only four days, and he was not completely stabilized. He got a ride from a friend to our home and proceeded to move as much of his belongings as possible out. He kept coming back to the house, and I kept calling the police on him. Finally, I got an order of protection. I was just heartbroken, and it only got worse. I had been going to the doctor for almost five months because I was having feminine problems; and so finally, I asked them to check me for venereal diseases it had gotten so bad. When I received that call from the nurse with my test results, I couldn't handle the news, so Suzzie did. She called him up first and let him have it then she went home and burnt everything he left in the house that she could fit in the fire pit, bags and bags, and bags of all his stuff. It had all been packed up to give to him.

I finally had my proof he was having an affair. My entire world came crashing down around me. The tornado had finally dissipated, and all the debris was falling down around me. I didn't want to breathe let alone move. I woke up every morning, sat up, and hung my legs over the side of the bed, took a deep breath in, and exhaled with I hate you. Every time I thought of him, I repeated this new ritual, deep breath in, exhale with I hate you. I was home and alone most of the time. I had just had carpal tunnel release surgery. Not only didn't I have the use of my dominant arm, I had nothing to occupy my time as I was on medical leave from both of my jobs. I cried so much my eyes were puffed shut most days, and I just continued to pick up the pieces. It was at his deep dark time in my life. I began reflecting back on my life and pieces just starting fitting right into place. It was all so clear to me now. My eyes were wide open. I had created all this, I had been perpetuating my cycle of abuse my entire life. I kept myself a victim for forty years, I had unknowingly made decisions over and over and over again that landed me in the same place every time. It was then that I realized the power I really hold. It was then that I realized the strength I truly possess, and it was then that I realized I had to change, if I wanted my life to change.

Now, I hadn't talked to my husband in weeks. I had sold my wedding ring and had divorce papers in hand. I don't know what came over me, but I texted him in the middle of the night one night. I told him that whenever he went down on me in bed, I had to fantasize about him having sex with other men to get off. If you ask me that was a Suzzie move. A couple of days later, something moved me to call him. We talked and agreed to meet in a couple of days. He had been taking his medications and sounded like himself again. I can only give our angels credit for what happened next. He told me he wasn't giving up on me, on us. He just couldn't. Just like he couldn't give up on me no matter how hard I pushed him away. I couldn't give up on him either. I let him come home, and we started rebuilding our lives together. We went to counseling together and worked hard to change in a positive direction. We changed for each other. We changed for our children and grandchildren; but most of all, we changed for ourselves. We both confessed our crimes against each other and agreed to work through it no matter how hard it was.

He jumped in the car and traveled with me so that I could make an attempt to fill in the missing pieces of my life. We drove to Tennessee to pay my eldest brother a visit. After all, he had come to meet me for the first time; so now, it was my turn to pay him a visit. Shout out Tennessee. What a beautiful place. A couple of months later, we jumped back in the car and drove to Michigan to visit four other of my siblings. Two of my sisters I didn't remember meeting when I had gone to visit them back in my twenties. As a matter of fact, the only thing I recall about the visit I had back then was meeting their mom and remembering how much I enjoyed her while I was there. The rest is a blank. I even have pictures of myself with them from that visit and those haven't helped trigger the memory back. So it was like meeting them for the first time. Let me tell you, they sure are one group of beautiful people, and the only word I can use to describe the feeling of having them in my life is blessed.

As I was talking with my oldest sister, and she was sharing her story with me, I realized that my story was indeed true. You see, all these years, I couldn't decipher the difference between flashbacks, dreams, memories. I couldn't tell if my life was just a made-up bad dream or reality. When she started talking, the confirmations started coming when she shared what was done to her. It matched up with what was done to me. I shared some of my flashbacks with her, and she confirmed them because he had done those same things to her.

Talk about mixed emotions. It was a relief to know that I wasn't indeed crazy rather a wounded soul.

When we returned from vacation, life got back to normal. Now, when John and I had split and got back together, he told me he had a one night stand; that was it and all. Now my intuition was telling me differently, but my heart wanted to believe, so I did.

Well, it was a beautiful sunny afternoon (as it always is when this stuff goes down, isn't it?). I was picking the kids up from school. I heard a little voice in my head as I was waiting in the car. "Look in the arm rest." So I looked. There was one of his old phones. I was debating on even looking because we just talked and healed, and I just wanted to move forward and trust, so I was thinking I'd just ask him about the phone. I picked it up and swiped it. *Boom*, it was the right code. I had now opened the phone. I was not one to got through phones in a relationship; I'd rather talk shit out. I thought, *Self, after ten years and all the bullshit, what do you have to lose?* So I looked, and I was about to pass out. Right in front of my eyes was evidence of an entire ongoing affair. So let me just tell you, folks, that things change in life at the drop of a dime.

Writing this memoir has been quite a healing journey for me. I've learned many things about myself I did not know, and there is still much more about myself that is kept secret. I didn't realize I was different growing up. I didn't know that losing time wasn't normal. I had no idea that everyone else didn't have other people living in their bodies with them. It was normal for me, normal all my life until just a couple of years ago. I started to put all the pieces together when I asked my sister what she thought about all of it. Her response was jaw dropping. "Well, yes. Don't you remember when you were in the hospital they said you had it, that multiple personality disorder." Even though I was asking her opinion, because I already had an idea that it was true, I immediately denied it. I denied it because I wasn't present during that hospital stay, and I truly did not remember. The medical records from the state facility were unobtainable as they had been shut down. Some of my records have been destroyed. My therapist of seven years asked me the other day why didn't I tell her about Suzzie. I responded by saying when I had spoken about her in the past I was placed on anti-psychotics to make her go away, but the truth of the matter is that Suzzie was my biggest secret. Most of my life, I was unaware that having Suzzie in me wasn't normal. I had grown up with her. She was always with me, and she still is to this day. She continues to keep me safe by keeping much of the abuse locked away, and only she holds the key. Yes, there is much I don't even know about myself, and that is okay with me.

It can be very easy to get caught up in feeling sorry for myself. After all, I have suffered unimaginable abuse, such unthinkable acts that I have not been able to reveal them to myself. I've lived my life unknowingly perpetuating that childhood abuse. I created situation after situation to keep myself in victim mode and keep the abuse going throughout my life. Unfortunately, this is a common side effect of childhood trauma; but the cycle can be broken. We don't have to live our lives in this perpetual cycle. We don't have to live as victims the rest of our lives. We were strong enough to survive. There are many who don't, but we did. We are strong. We are survivors, and that my friends is what we must celebrate.

Now is the time to break the silence and set our secrets free because when we do this, it gives us back our power, the power that was taken from us against our will. We must talk about sexual abuse, sexual harassment, and sexual misconduct. This is the only way to stop it. If it's not acknowledged, it can't be addressed. We need to call our abusers out, and make them accountable. Not only for ourselves but for every other woman and child we are saving from them by speaking out.

When I read my own story, I have a hard time digesting that it is indeed my story, my life; and these are my truths. I don't want it to be mine. I never wanted it to be my story. I spent years trying to bring my story to an end. I am a firm believer that everything happens for a reason and believing that is what brought me here, to you. I want to move you. If you have a similar story, tell it. If you know someone who has been through abuse, share my story so they won't feel alone. If you or anyone you know have not been affected by abuse, reach out to those who have. This is an epidemic of phenomenal proportions, which is permeated by secrecy. We need to stand up, open our eyes, our mouths, and most of all our hearts. If you see something suspicious, say something. If you hear something suspicious, acknowledge it, and investigate it. Don't sweep it under the rug and ignore it because you could be saving someone from a horrible situation they can't save themselves from or better yet, you could be saving a life.

We are all brothers and sisters. All our souls are connected, and we are supposed to take care of each other. If you were walking down the street and an elderly woman fell to the ground, you wouldn't walk past her and think, *Oh, someone else will notice and help her*; or *I don't have time to get involved with that*. You would stop and help her up. You would make sure she was okay. Victims of abuse deserve that same level of compassion. So I'm asking you to educate yourselves, know what signs to look for, and don't turn your head away for the fear of being uncomfortable. I know that I wanted so badly to be saved. I begged and pleaded to god to send someone to rescue me, and it never happened. No one ever showed up to wrap me up in their arms, to rock me, to hold me, and to tell me it was over and everything would be okay. I wanted someone to notice my pain, and no one ever did. I won't lie. This has been one of the most difficult tasks in my life. There hasn't been one time that I have sat down to write that I didn't shed tears. When I start to feel sorry for myself, I allow those feeling to come; and I am present with them. What I have learned is to not get stuck in these feelings. This too shall pass, and it does. I have learned to ride the waves of life so that I don't get caught in the undertow.

There are a few things I need you to know before we part ways. Know your worth. No matter what your story is or what you have been through, know that you are important and loveable. When you are in that dark place that has you contemplating suicide, reach out because there is a beautiful life waiting for you on the other side of that dark place. If you are feeling like there is no one in the world who loves you, know that I love you. Know that it is truly okay to not be okay sometimes. It's okay to lose your composure, cry uncontrollably, and scream at the top of your lungs when the emotional pain is overwhelming. It's part of the healing process. Know that healing is a process and one that never ends, and that is a good thing. It is a gift we can give ourselves as survivors. To heal is to learn, and we never want to stop learning. Know that you can be gentle and patient with yourself because you deserve it. Please know that you have choices, and you are in control of your own life. Know that you have a voice, and you are empowered to speak up and speak out. Know that great things take time, hard work and change; but it is oh so worth it! Last but definitely not least, know who you are; and know that you are beautiful.

I myself am a daughter, a sister, a loving mother, an aunt, and a proud grandmother. I am a believer in the power of love, a champion of my own demise. I am a cousin, a caregiver, a servant to the public, and an artist. I am a lover, a fighter for what I believe in, and an eternal optimist. I am the bearer of a mental illness caused by childhood trauma. I am a humble woman who has bared her soul to you. Most of all, I am a survivor of a ferocious thunderstorm who has finally found her rainbow.

Child sexual abuse hotline
1-866 FOR LIGHT (1-866-367-5444)

National Child abuse hotline
1-800 4 A CHILD (1-800-422-4453)

RAINN—Rape, Abuse, and Incest National Network
1-800-656-HOPE (1-800-656-4673)

NAMI—National Alliance on Mental Illness
1-800-950-NAMI (1-800-950-6264)

National sexual assault hotline
1-800-656=4673

National suicide prevention hotline
1-800-273-TALK (1-800-273-8255)

Domestic abuse hotline
1-800-799-SAFE (1-800-799-7233)

National Alcohol and Substance abuse information center.
1-800-784-6776

ABOUT THE AUTHOR

Pamela Devereueawax is a funeral director and embalmer by trade, but her true passion has always been in the literary arts. She began writing poetry and short stories early in life. As she became older, she realized she possessed a gift, one that she knew must be shared with the world; so she embarked on her journey to become a published author.

The genre that best describes her work is inspirational. Pamela is a passionate humanitarian who has volunteered her time to work at local women's shelters, completed training for sexual assault crisis counseling, and was a licensed foster parent for a number of years. Pamela currently resides in northern Illinois with her loving husband of five years. She is the proud mother of eight, adoring grandmother of six, and loving pet mommy of two pit bull terriers. When she is not busy caring for our dearly departed or creating her next work of art, she enjoys gardening, researching astrology, and traveling. Pamela has had the privilege of traveling all over the world, which has given her experiences of a lifetime. You will want to make sure you keep your eye out for her up and coming literary works. To connect with Pamela Devereueawax, just look her up on Facebook and Instagram.